Your

BOOK THREE

CHOICE

JOHN FOSTER, SIMON FOSTER & KIM RICHARDSON

Collins

William Collins' dream of knowledge for all began with the publication of his first book in 1819.

A self-educated mill worker, he not only enriched millions of lives, but also founded a flourishing publishing house. Today, staying true to this spirit, Collins books are packed with inspiration, innovation and practical expertise. They place you at the centre of a world of possibility and give you exactly what you need to explore it.

Collins. Freedom to teach.

Published by Collins

An imprint of HarperCollins*Publishers*

The News Building
1 London Bridge Street
London
SE1 9GF

HarperCollins *Publishers*
Macken House, 39/40 Mayor Street Upper,
Dublin 1, D01 C9W8, Ireland

Browse the complete Collins catalogue at
www.collins.co.uk

10 9 8 7 6 5 4

ISBN 978-0-00-832899-3

British Library Cataloguing in Publication Data

A catalogue record for this publication is available from the British Library.

The publishers would like to thank the following for their help in reviewing the series:
- Jo Fliski, formerly Head of PSHE and English teacher at Lliswerry High School, Newport
- Jo Haycock, Psychology teacher at Sir John Talbot's School, Whitchurch, Shropshire and formerly PSHE Coordinator at Newport Girls' High School
- Tara Mellor, teacher of PSHE, Citizenship and Law, The Mirfield Free Grammar and Sixth Form
- Cat Crossley, diversity consultant and publisher.

Series editor: John Foster
Development editor: Jo Kemp
Commissioning editor: Catherine Martin
Copyeditor: Jo Kemp
Proofreader: Karen Williams
Cover designer: The Big Mountain
Concept designer: The Big Mountain
Internal designer / Typesetter: 2Hoots Publishing Services Ltd
Permissions researcher: Rachel Thorne
Production controller: Katharine Willard
Printed by Ashford Colour Press Ltd

Contents

Introduction

Your Choice Book Three is the third of three books which together form a comprehensive course in Personal, Social and Health Education (PSHE), including Relationships and Sex Education (RSE) and Health Education, at Key Stage 3. The table shows how the topics covered fit within four strands – Personal wellbeing and mental health, Relationships and sex, Physical health and wellbeing and Social education – could provide a coherent course in RSE and PSHE for students in Year 9. Each unit could also be taught on its own, at any point during Key Stage 3 that your school thinks is appropriate.

The units provide you with key information on relevant topics and the various activities provide opportunities for you to share your views and to develop your own opinions.

Throughout the book there are discussion activities that involve you in learning how to work as a team and how to develop the skills of co-operation and negotiation. You are presented with situations in which you must work with others, to analyse information, to consider what actions you could take and to make choices and decisions.

Personal wellbeing and mental health

These units focus on developing your confidence and self-esteem, on managing your mental health and on the negative effects gambling can have on your life.

Relationships and sex education

These units concentrate on your developing sexuality and gender, your rights including LGBTQ+ rights, helping you stay safe at parties and online. They also offer support on becoming pregnant and explore parenthood, marriage and partnership.

Each lesson has a clear focus.

Fact check boxes highlight key facts and statistics.

Engaging and varied activities will check your understanding and ask you to develop and express your own views in discussion, writing and through further research.

Articles, poems and images provide a stimulus for discussion and help you to understand other people's viewpoints and experiences.

Realistic scenarios help you to explore issues safely.

Physical health and wellbeing

These units focus on coping with social pressures online, on eating disorders and on the dangers of drugs and drug taking, in particular taking heroin and cocaine.

- **6** Drugs and drug taking
- **9** Social pressures
- **10** Eating disorders

Social education

These units explore racism at school, at work and in society; gangs and knife crime; fake news, radicalisation and online literacy; your rights as a consumer; and the global issues of climate change, poverty and genetic engineering.

- **4** Racism, prejudice and discrimination
- **11** Young people and crime
- **12** Fake news, radicalisation and online literacy
- **16** Global issues

1.1 Building your confidence

Confidence is concerned with how we feel about ourselves and our abilities.

How confidence affects us

Being confident can make a big difference to how happy and effective we are in life. Low confidence, by contrast, can hold us back.

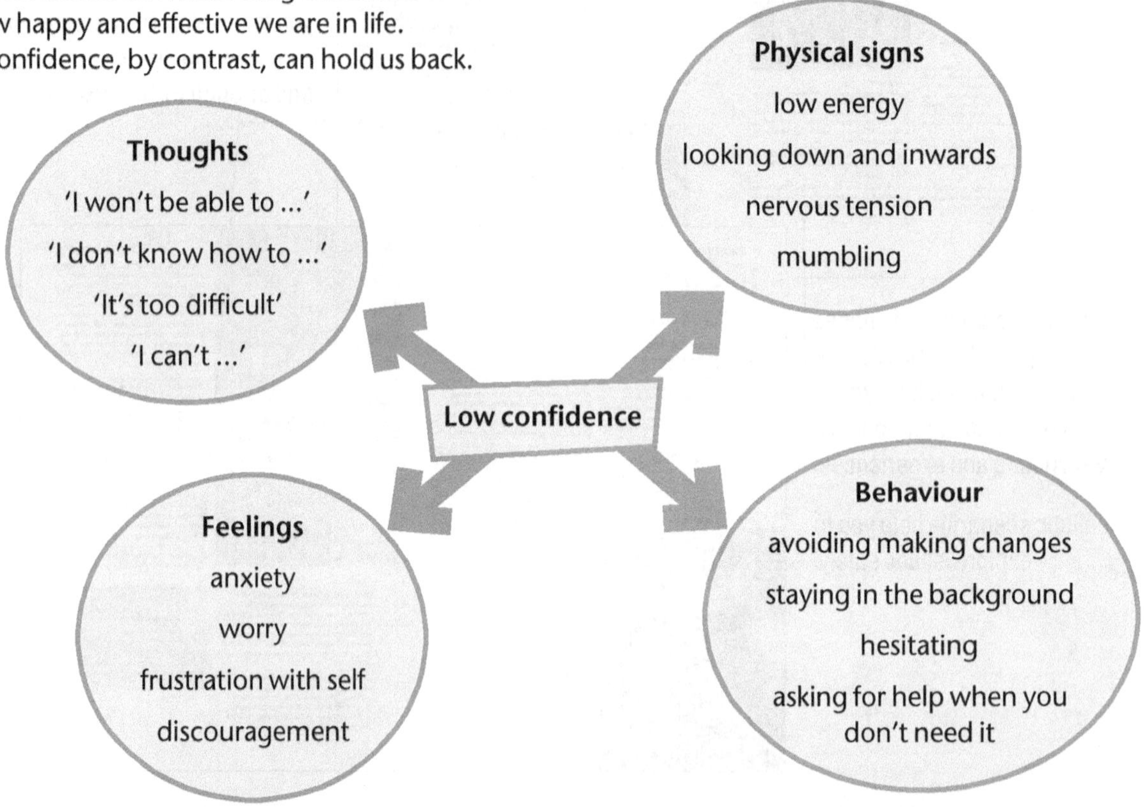

Thoughts

'I won't be able to ...'

'I don't know how to ...'

'It's too difficult'

'I can't ...'

Physical signs

low energy

looking down and inwards

nervous tension

mumbling

Low confidence

Feelings

anxiety

worry

frustration with self

discouragement

Behaviour

avoiding making changes

staying in the background

hesitating

asking for help when you don't need it

WRITE

1. Look at the diagram above. Think about an area where you have low confidence, perhaps when you are at a party, or when you are given a difficult task to do. Write down the thoughts, feelings and behaviours that may be holding you back from achieving what you want.

2. Think about an area where you are more confident. What thoughts, feelings and behaviours help you achieve what you want? Draw up a diagram.

RESEARCH

1. Ask friends and family members about confidence.

   • What are they confident about, and where do they feel low in confidence?

   • What thoughts, feelings and behaviours hold them back, and which help them?

2. Write a short statement outlining what you have learned about confidence from your research.

DISCUSS

Discuss the writing task above with a partner. How could you use the same thoughts, feelings and behaviours in situation 2 to help you in situation 1?

Boosting your confidence

Colin Letts offers some tips

Think positively. Those 'I can't ...' and 'What if ...?' thoughts really hold you back. If you expect something will turn out badly then it's more likely to go wrong – or not to happen at all. Practise some positive thinking instead, for instance, 'It will help if I ...' or, 'It'll be fine.'

Behave 'as if'. Sometimes you need to act confidently in order to learn confidence. Very few people are naturally 100 per cent confident. So, imagine confidence is a suit of clothes, and put it on. Hold your head high, make eye contact, speak up, be decisive – and see what happens.

Have a go. Try to do some new things. Confidence is something that can be learned, but you can only learn it by practising. That means taking risks sometimes. Whether or not you succeed, people will appreciate that you gave it a go, and the more you practise, the easier it will become.

Learn from your mistakes. It's not the end of the world if you give a wrong answer in class or belly flop when showing off your diving skills. Everyone makes mistakes. But don't just put it behind you – learn from where you went wrong and get better!

Take one step at a time. Don't set unrealistic targets which mean you will always fail. Set small goals for yourself – ones you can achieve. Taking a step-by-step approach will build the foundations for greater confidence in the long run.

Tara's story

Fifteen-year-old Tara from Southampton used to be terrified of the water. When her brothers were learning to sail, she would stay on shore and feel bad about herself.

'I wanted to have a go, but was frightened of looking stupid if I couldn't do it,' she said. 'But one day I thought, "If I fall in, I can swim, can't I?" and I just went for it. I joined the beginner's course, which took things really slowly. Of course, it wasn't all easy, but I loved it and kept at it.'

Now Tara has a Start Sailing qualification, and is helping out at her local Yachting Association events. It's been a turning point in her life. 'I'm so proud of myself,' she said. 'It has given me the confidence to try out other things too.'

DISCUSS

1. Read Colin Letts's advice on boosting your confidence and Tara's story above.

   a) Which piece of advice is the most useful?

   b) What strategies did Tara use to build her confidence?

2. 'Only those who dare to fail greatly can ever achieve greatly.' (Robert F. Kennedy)

   What did Robert Kennedy mean? How can you fail greatly?

YOUR CHOICE

What advice would you give to Aaron, Chrissie and Dwayne?

'I am too shy to put my hand up in class.' Aaron

'I don't go to parties because I won't know what to say to people.' Chrissie

'I want to learn how to cook, but I'll never be as good as my dad.' Dwayne

1.2 Self-esteem

Self-esteem is different from confidence.

Why self-esteem is important

Confidence is mainly about believing in your abilities, but even very confident people can feel that they are not good enough *in themselves*. Self-esteem is about valuing and accepting *yourself*, whatever your achievements. So, building self-esteem is like building a foundation for a house, which will allow it to stand solid and strong whatever the circumstances. It is the basis for enjoyment and success in life.

Myths that lower our self-esteem

MYTH 1: *You can only value yourself if you are good at things.*

TRUTH: We are all worthy of love and value, just for being human. Do you value your friends for their achievements, or because they are them? Use the same standard to be kind to yourself.

MYTH 2: *Valuing yourself is arrogant.*

TRUTH: Arrogance is putting yourself above other people in an unfair way, or having an exaggerated opinion of yourself. Valuing yourself and others is being fair to yourself and accepting yourself for who you are.

MYTH 3: *The approval of others is more important than valuing yourself.*

TRUTH: Usually, we are only dependent on others for our good feelings about ourselves when we don't have those feelings. It's an insecure place to be, because other people's judgements change. It is better to value yourself than to rely on the approval of others.

How to build self-esteem – the four keys

🔑 Recognise your strengths

One way to build your self-esteem is to make a list of your qualities, skills, talents and strengths. This will help to develop your positive sense of yourself, and bring to mind things that you may not generally notice about yourself.

Under the heading 'My positive qualities', simply list as many good things about yourself as you can. Give yourself time to do this, and make sure you are relaxed and alone when you do it. Add things to the list as the days pass. Enjoy seeing it build up, and read it frequently.

🔑 Challenge the inner critic

There is often a judge or critic inside you putting you down whatever your achievements. 'She'll do it better', 'I'm rubbish', 'It was only luck', 'It's all my fault', 'I always mess up' – you know the sorts of things the critic says.

The inner critic is just a series of automatic thoughts that you have developed since childhood. It is usually unfair, harsh and exaggerated. Learn to challenge it – or just not to listen to it. Try to speak to yourself as you would to someone you care about.

Beware of perfectionism

Many people think that it is good to be a perfectionist – to want to be as perfect as possible in everything you do. But this can cause a lot of problems, for example putting something off – or not doing it at all – because 'it won't be good enough'. Above all, it undermines your self-esteem because usually we are *not* perfect – so according to the standard of perfectionism, we are failures.

A better rule to follow is simply to do the best you can.

Feel good about being yourself

Be yourself. Don't try to act and think in a particular way just to be popular or safe. People will see through you – and you won't like yourself for it.

Instead, think about what *you* want and what *you* believe in. What do you like to do and who do you like to spend time with? How can you increase the time you spend with people who make you feel good? The more you are yourself, the more you will be happy with the way you are.

> I hang around with all the cool people at school and wear what they wear, but I'm still not accepted. How can I make myself more popular?
>
> **Riley**

> However well I do at school, it's never good enough. I get top marks but can't enjoy that because I'm afraid of failing next time. It makes me so unhappy.
>
> **Jess**

DISCUSS

Read 'How to build self-esteem – the four keys'.

1. In pairs, discuss the advice the article gives.

2. What sorts of things does your own inner critic say? Think about times when you are unhappy with yourself, or when your confidence is low.

3. Get your partner to help you challenge the unfairness, the exaggeration, the negative predictions. For example, this is how Harry challenges his inner critic when he has had an argument with his parents:

Inner critic:

> I can't do anything right. Mum and dad are always down on me.

Challenge:

> I do lots of things right at home, like when I helped wash up yesterday. And mum and dad didn't get at me when I broke my phone.

WRITE

The posts above were made on an online teenage forum. Write a reply to Riley or Jess.

YOUR CHOICE

Look at the statements below. Think about whether you agree or disagree with each one and why. Then share your views with a partner.

> The best way to boost your self-esteem is to behave like the most popular people in your class. Cara

> Self-esteem is just thinking you're great. Dan

> It's not how good you are at different things that matters; it's what kind of person you are underneath. Amar

> It's more important to do the best you can than to be perfect. Sasha

9

1.3 Coping with challenges and change

The teenage years are a time of massive change, physically and emotionally, with lots of ups and downs.

Teenage pressures

It's not easy being a teenager. As well as dealing with physical and emotional changes, and everything that is going on with your hormones, there are lots of external pressures. There is constant pressure from the internet and other media about how you should look and what you should be doing. There can be an unhelpful emphasis on perfection and winning. For all these reasons, it is not surprising that teenagers can lack self-esteem, or feel unable to cope when challenging things happen.

There might also be other changes in our lives. Parents separate. People get ill. Friends blow hot and cold. You fail an exam, or lose a job. We are all going to face stressful events in our lives. It's how we cope with them that makes the difference between crumpling under the pressure or dealing with the problems and getting on with our lives.

Building resilience

Sometimes people can go through really rough times and still bounce back – that's because they are using the skills of resilience. Resilience is the ability to adapt well in the face of hard times – and it can be learned. Here are some tips to help you build your resilience.

1. **Communicate.** Talk about your problems with your friends and family. Ask questions and listen to the answers. Don't cut yourself off, but keep connected. If talking is too hard at the moment, then just spend good quality time with people who matter. Or channel your emotions in other ways, like through music.

2. **Take care of yourself.** When something bad happens in your life, the extra stress on top of 'just living' can be very demanding. So be kind to yourself. Make sure you get enough sleep, and don't demand perfect standards of thought or behaviour.

3. **Stick to a routine.** When life seems chaotic and uncertain, it's really helpful to identify some fixed points to anchor you. Map out a routine and stick to it. This may just be the things you do before class, or the regular phone call with a friend. Find somewhere free from stress and anxieties that can act as a haven, a shelter from the storm – perhaps your room at home, or a friend's house.

4. **Take control.** Challenging times make us feel out of control, so you need to take some of that control back. That may mean decisive action, such as ending a relationship. Or it may mean taking much smaller steps. Even getting out of bed and going to school can be a cha llenge sometimes, so aim for that and notch it up as an achievement.

5. **Keep the problem in perspective.** It's easy to assume that the worst will happen, or has already happened. Ask yourself, 'Will this matter in a year from now?' Everything changes, which means that all bad times end. If you feel you are not up to the challenge, think of a time when you faced up to a different challenge, such as asking someone on a date. Don't just talk or think about the bad times; make sure you talk and think about good times too.

6. **Seek help when you need it.** If you are really struggling and these tips are not enough, seek help from a teacher, trusted adult or GP. They will be able to advise you and help you to get professional support if needed.

Coping with friendship issues

Peer-group issues can cause a lot of stress during adolescence, when friends become very important in our lives. The classroom is alive with competition, comparison and issues of status, which can make life very stressful. Writer Juno Dawson gives this advice:

There is no easy answer for remedying peer-group issues or the stress they cause. I do think this though: humans can never BELONG to other humans, and very often OWNERSHIP of friends seems to be an issue – 'You're MY friend, not HERS!', that sort of thing.

Friends come and go. Not a popular topic of any film or book you've ever seen, but the cold, hard truth. Some friendships are toxic to poisonous levels, and no friend is worth damaging your health over. Here's another truth: you'll make new friends. Honestly! You will!! As people change and evolve, you look for people with similar interests and outlooks. Over your teens and into your twenties, people will inevitably come and go, and that, as they say, is life.

So don't be afraid to opt out of a damaging friendship group. The only person you can control is you. Be fun, friendly and, most importantly, be KIND. Do that and you'll be a brilliant friend who attracts other NEW, fun, friendly, kind people. Don't let toxicity infect you. That's ALL you can do.

From Juno Dawson, *Mind Your Head*

DISCUSS

Think back to a time when your confidence or self-esteem was knocked, or you were under stress. Discuss with a partner what strategies you used to help you through that time.

- Which of the tips in the article did you use?
- Would you deal with things any differently now?

WRITE

Write a short statement beginning: 'When times are hard, remember these three key things ...'

DISCUSS

Read 'Coping with friendship issues'.

1. Do you agree with Juno Dawson's advice? Why or why not?

2. How does her advice relate to the tips on resilience given in 'Building resilience'?

3. Is opting out of a damaging friendship group 'ALL you can do'? What else could you do if your friend or friends criticise or bully you?

ROLE PLAY

'My friends can make me feel like I'm worthless. They make comments about my clothes and appearance. Not all the time, but it's enough to reduce me to tears.' Olivia

Role play a scene where one of you is Olivia and the other is someone giving her advice.

1.4 Problem-solving

The challenges and changes in our lives often cause us problems, so problem-solving is a very useful skill to have.

The bad news is that each problem is different. The good news is that we can learn a simple technique to tackle each problem in the most effective way.

Solve your problems – the S×4 way

Life throws lots of problems at us, some bigger than others, writes Addison Clarke.

Even the small problems can cause us a lot of stress if they matter a lot to us, or if we agonise over them. So having a strategy to solve problems is a powerful weapon in your armoury. It will build your confidence in tackling all sorts of issues – practical or emotional, at home or at school.

Try the S×4 method of problem-solving. The four steps are:

> **S**tate the problem
>
> List possible **S**olutions
>
> **S**elect the best solution
>
> **S**ee how it works.

It's simple but effective! Let's explore the four steps in more detail.

State the problem

It may seem obvious, but you can't do anything without identifying the problem. Try to state the problem as clearly as possible. Make sure it is something that is in your control. 'My sister is being a nightmare' isn't really a solvable problem. However, 'How can I manage my sister's behaviour?' is more in your control.

This is how Nathan stated his problem:

'I'm always short of money to do the things I want, and to buy the stuff I need.'

List possible solutions

Think of as many solutions as possible to your problem, and write them down. It's important that you don't criticise any of the solutions at this stage, however silly they sound. Be as creative as possible! If you find it hard to come up with ideas, ask a friend to help suggest things.

This is the list that Nathan wrote, with his friend's help:

- ask for a bigger weekly allowance from my parents
- look for a job
- sell some of my clothes on eBay
- borrow money from friends
- go out less
- ask for money for my birthday (though it's not for three months).

Select the best solution

Now choose the best solution. A good way to start is to rule out solutions that are unworkable, or that have too many disadvantages. Sometimes it helps to list the advantages and disadvantages of your proposed solutions. Again, discussing the solutions with a friend can be very useful. You may end up with more than one good solution. If so, you could have a Plan A and a back-up Plan B in case your chosen solution fails. Or you could try both.

Nathan crossed off his list 'ask for a bigger weekly allowance' because he knew his existing allowance was already generous. He also ruled out 'borrow money from friends' because he'd got into trouble with that before. He thought selling clothes wouldn't bring in very much money. Out of the other solutions, getting a job seemed to be the best. 'I saw that a cafe round the corner was looking for someone to work in the kitchen. And our neighbours are always looking for babysitters.'

See how it works

Now it's time to put your chosen solution into effect. That means having a plan of action. Sometimes plans can consist of several careful steps; sometimes it's just a matter of plucking up courage and saying what you want. In either case, evaluate what happens. If it's successful, keep doing it. If it's not, work out what went wrong and adjust the solution or try another solution from your list.

'I didn't get the cafe job,' said Nathan, 'but I leafleted lots of neighbours about babysitting and I've already got two promises. That's money for playing with the kids and watching TV!'

Dos and don'ts

The S×4 method is remarkably straightforward. If you get stuck, maybe these rules will help.

Write things down. It's useful to discuss things with a friend or someone you live with, but there is no substitute for listing all possible solutions. You can't do this in your head!

Don't waste time on unsolvable problems. See 'State the problem' above.

Don't avoid the problem. It may seem easier at the time just to buy your head in the sand. However, often this can make the problem bigger in the long run, and even cause other problems along the way.

You may need more help. If your problem is causing huge stress or trouble for you, you may need other resources. If, for example you are too depressed or anxious to solve your problems effectively on your own, you should talk to a trusted adult or seek help from a GP.

DISCUSS

A. Joey is worried that he's spending too much time on social media sites. He is often unable to focus on anything else, and he is often on edge. He doesn't sleep well because he checks his phone so much through the night.

B. Charlie is getting more and more spiteful comments about her appearance from her friendship group. The comments focus on her skin and hair and they often reduce her to tears. The situation seemed to get worse when a new girl, Nadine, joined the group.

In groups, choose one of the scenarios above and use the S×4 method to help Joey or Charlie tackle their problem.

ROLE PLAY

With a partner, role play one of these two problems, with one of you the person with the problem and the other giving advice. Then swap roles and role play the other problem.

1. I want to become a vegan but I know it will stress my dad out when he cooks for the family.

2. I'm always so disorganised in the morning. I often miss the bus or leave things behind that I need for school.

YOUR CHOICE

On your own, identify a problem that is worrying you at the moment. Use the S×4 method to find a good solution.

2.1 Your developing sexuality

Puberty is a time when feelings about sex and sexuality become particularly important. This happens at different times for different people, and it can be very changeable and confusing.

The bottom line is that sexuality is an individual thing. You are allowed to be who you are.

Below, some 18 year olds look back on their early teen experiences:

'My hormones were really racing. I couldn't get sex out of my mind. It was exciting but horrible at the same time, like I wasn't in charge of my feelings.' **Leanne**

'Even before secondary school I felt I was a boy and wanted to do "boys' things". When I hit puberty those feelings rocketed, and I began to identify as trans. I was physically attracted to boys and girls, which was confusing at first.' **Sam**

'There was a lot of pressure to have a girlfriend. My friends did a lot of bragging about how far they'd gone with girls, although later I realised they were making a lot of this up. I felt left behind, but also quite relieved I wasn't part of it.' **Jack**

DISCUSS

Discuss what you learn from the young people's comments about how we express ourselves sexually.

1. What is the difference between loving someone and being sexually attracted to them?

2. What advice would you have given to Leanne if you had been her friend at the time?

3. What sort of feelings might Raj have had about his sexual development?

'I could see that boys in my class were getting more and more interested in girls, but I just wanted to write songs and play my guitar. Luckily, most of my close friends felt the same as me. It took time, and that was OK.' **Raj**

'I got too involved with a boy too soon and regret that now. I didn't realise that being sexually attracted to someone is very different from loving them.' **Bethan**

'I had a crush on my male art teacher in Year 7. I used to invent scenes in my head where we'd be together. It was pretty innocent though – an early sign of my feelings for guys which came out a couple of years later.' **Ben**

Coming out

Colin Letts explores the choices that young people have.

The sexual desires that you have are not something that you choose.

The choice you *do* have is when and how you want to act on those feelings.

Maybe you don't want to act on your feelings. You think they are just part of a whole range of sexual feelings that are racing through you at puberty. Or it's just too scary to act on them. Or your family or religion tells you they are wrong, or that they don't even exist.

You may be able to continue like this for a while, but usually, where there is a clash between what you feel and what you or your family or your religion tells you that you should feel, you end up very unhappy. Or stressed, or behaving badly. Or a combination of these things.

'I kept a lid on my feelings for other girls for a long time. I didn't want to acknowledge them. What would my friends and family say? But I just felt this terrible pressure inside, and hated living a lie.' Gilda (14)

Maybe you do want to act on the feelings. You think it's okay to date someone of the same gender as you. (You're right, it is!) Or to date people of different genders. (Right again!) You may also be happy experimenting with make-up or clothes. It's all part of the varied spectrum of sexual expression.

'It was so liberating when I started letting in the fact that I fancied girls and boys. I just kept it simple and followed my feelings.' Marilla (15)

Maybe you are ready to define yourself as gay or lesbian or bi. You are confident about how you feel and you see these feelings as a central part of your identity. They become an essential element of who you are and how you lead your life – how you present yourself to the world, and to yourself. This can be an exciting and revolutionary time in your development as a human being.

'It isn't enough to tell people that I am gay. I want to hang around with other gay guys and really work out what it means for me to be gay. The gay scene gives me safety and a supportive community as well as identity.' Mike (17)

DISCUSS

1. What different ways of expressing your feelings and/or coming out does Colin Letts describe in the article?
2. If a young person wants to come out as gay, lesbian or bi, what might they need to think about first?

Ask Erica

Dear Erica
I am having fantasies about girls. I am really confused by this.
Monique (15)

Dear Erica
I am having fantasies about boys. Does that mean I'm gay or bisexual? Should I come out?'
Sajid (14)

Dear Erica
I always thought I was gay, but now I am having fantasies about this guy. What's going on?'
Tess (15)

WRITE

Write Erica's reply to Monique, Sajid or Tess.

2.2 What influences your attitudes to sexuality and gender?

Thinking about where our attitudes come from helps us become more understanding, both of ourselves and of others.

Thinking about our influences

'My friends and I spend so much time talking about girls. There's a group energy that's very powerful and a bit scary.' **Connor**

'The church I go to is very supportive towards gay people, so I am very lucky.' **Michele**

'I think we are pressurised by the media about how men and women should behave. It's sex, sex, sex, isn't it?' **Chris**

'Because of my religion, my parents expect me not to have sex until I'm married. That's hard for me when the standards are different for my friends.' **Simran**

YOUR CHOICE

What factors influence your own views and behaviour around sexuality and gender? Think about what the young people above have said, and about your own family, friends, culture and religion. Also think about the media, especially social media. Rate these factors in order of importance, then, if you wish, compare your answers with others in the group.

The man box

Educator and activist Tony Porter talks about how he and other men like him were brought up (or 'socialised') to have a rigid and unhealthy picture of manhood. He describes it as the 'man box', which has all the ingredients of what it means to be a man.

Don't cry or openly express emotions (except anger)

Don't show weakness or fear

Demonstrate power/control (especially over women)

Aggression–Dominance

Protector

Do not be 'like a woman'

Heterosexual

Do not be 'like a gay man'

Tough–Athletic–Strength–Courage

Makes decisions – does not need help

Views women as property/objects

DISCUSS

1. What do you think counts as 'normal' (a) for being a man, (b) for being a woman in your society today? Where do we learn this?

2. What do you think are the consequences of males being brought up in the man box?

3. A lot of women also feel that they have been brought up with a rigid idea of what it means to be a woman. What do you think would be in this 'woman box'?

YOUR CHOICE

Imagine you could take men and women out of their boxes. What characteristics of manhood/womanhood would you like society to encourage? Would you, in fact, make any distinction between men and women?

Pornography

The problem with porn

by Jez Franks

Porn. It's everywhere. Because the internet is everywhere and nonstop. So, it's sex education at your fingertips. But what kind of education are you getting? To begin with, you don't learn about the part sex plays in building relationships. The relationships portrayed in heterosexual porn are usually those where women are sex objects – they are dominated and often humiliated by men, and issues of consent are often ignored. Research shows that people who watch a lot of pornography can have more difficulty forming relationships. Porn doesn't teach you about love and feelings, and it lowers your sensitivity to partner violence – especially violence against women.

Even the sex that is portrayed in porn is unrealistic. How real are the men's and women's bodies? How often do you see a condom being used? How many people in real life actually take part in group sex or dangerous sex acts? How much talking and cuddling and touching is portrayed? Porn presents a distorted picture of sex and makes it seem 'normal'. Remember that these are actors performing in a film – so it's made up. It's an industry, designed to make money – at your expense.

It's also a very male-dominated industry. Most porn is made for men by men. This can have a huge effect on what boys expect: boys may assume they have to be hyper-masculine, and that girls want the kind of treatment they see acted out online. Increasingly, young people are complaining that their partners are expecting them to look or act like porn stars.

Return to the idea at the start of this article. Can porn be seen as sex education? Only if a drug dealer teaching you about drugs is education. Let's call it something else – harmful indoctrination.

Fact check

Porn and the law

- It is unlawful for under-18s to buy pornographic magazines, view explicit images or watch explicit videos.

- It is unlawful for under-18s to send explicit messages, photos or films of themselves or of other young people.

- Possessing images and portrayals of acts that are defined as 'extreme pornography' is illegal, even for adults. These include degrading or violent porn, or porn involving people under 18 years old.

DISCUSS

1. Read 'The problem with porn' and then discuss the views of Dafydd and Nat below.

   'Pornography helps young people learn about sex.' **Dafydd**

   'Pornography leads to unrealistic and harmful attitudes to sex.' **Nat**

2. How else can you learn about sex as a young person?

3. How might porn make a young person feel about their sexuality or their gender identity? *(See Unit 2.3 for more about your gender identity.)*

4. Porn is overwhelmingly used by men. Why do you think this is?

2.3 Understanding gender identity

Some young people are comfortable with the gender they were assigned at birth. Some young people do not feel their gender identity is the same as their biological sex. These feelings may intensify before or during puberty and lead to a young person wanting to change or express their gender identity in a different way.

Fact check

- **Sex** refers to the biology of being male or female.

- **Sexuality** refers to your sexual preference, feelings and behaviour.

- **Gender** refers to the roles and behaviours that society sets up as 'normal' for men and women.

- **Gender identity** refers to how someone feels about or expresses their gender.

- **Cis or cisgender** is where your gender identity is the same as your biological sex.

- **Trans** is an umbrella term referring to someone whose gender does not sit comfortably with the sex they were assigned at birth.

- **Non-binary** is an umbrella term referring to gender identities that are not exclusively 'masculine' or 'feminine'.

- **Gender fluid** refers to someone who does not identify themselves as having a fixed gender.

- **LGBT+ and LGBTQ** are umbrella terms used to describe people who do not identify as heterosexual or cisgender: L = lesbian, G = gay, B = bisexual, T = transgender, Q = queer, + refers to other identities, for example intersex or asexual.

- **Intersex** refers to people who may have the biological attributes of both sexes or who do not completely fit into the categories 'male' or 'female'; they may identify as male, female or non-binary.

DISCUSS

Read the definitions of the terms for sexuality and gender identity above. Then discuss the following questions:

1. What is the difference between sexuality and gender identity?

2. Why is this important?

Myths about being trans

There is a lot of confusion around what being trans means. There's also prejudice and misinformation.

MYTH 1: *The world is divided into men and women. End of.*

TRUTH: It's not as simple as that; some people identify as trans, gender fluid or non-binary. The spectrum of different gender identities includes anyone who doesn't feel comfortable with the gender they were assigned (given) at birth or who feels they don't fit neatly into the two categories 'male' and female'.

MYTH 2: *Being transgender is just a trendy choice.*

TRUTH: Some young people's gender identity matches the sex into which they were born. But for some people it doesn't match. Identifying as different from your birth sex can cause feelings of great distress and discomfort because of society's expectations. Identifying as transgender is no more of a choice than identifying as straight or Black.

MYTH 3: *Being transgender is just a phase – it is something a young person will grow out of.*

TRUTH: In some cases, the feelings may be temporary and the young person does not continue to identify as trans. But at adolescence the feelings can intensify for some people, rather than going away. In both cases, the person's feelings and aspirations need to be taken seriously and supported.

MYTH 4: *If you are trans it means you want to have surgery to change your biology.*

TRUTH: Trans is an umbrella term that covers a range of experiences. There is never a one-size-fits-all approach. Some people want to change their gender through surgery or hormone treatment, but not everyone does. Other people want to live their lives in and be recognised as the gender with which they identify. It's more about the person doing what makes them feel comfortable and true to themselves.

MYTH 5: *Transgender identities aren't normal. They'll never be real men or women.*

TRUTH: Everybody is different whether they are trans or not. Trans women are women and trans men are men.

MYTH 6: *Trans people are gay.*

TRUTH: Being trans is about gender, not sexuality. Like anyone else, trans people can be gay, or straight, or bi, or whatever works for them.

Zayn's story

From as early as I can remember I felt that I was a girl. But I was told not to play with girls or wear anything girly. And my school also tried to make me conform. So I guess I suppressed my feelings for years. But when my voice broke and I started getting body hair and all the rest, I was forced to address my real identity. It was a horrible time because I was terrified of being thrown out by my family. Often I felt desperate. I called a helpline and they gave me amazing emotional and practical support. I just want to be happy with myself and live life as the real me.

Jess's story

As a child, I didn't have a strong sense of my own gender. I never got the whole 'girl' and 'boy' thing. I've always felt that I'm a bit of both. I was sort of OK with this, and my parents never tried to push me one way or the other. But when my breasts started growing, I really freaked out. We've had a lot of help from support groups. I'm realising that I'm gender fluid – and that's OK!

How to support a friend who is questioning their gender identity

A school counsellor writes ...

It can be hard to know how to respond when a close friend tells you they are trans, non-binary or exploring their gender identity. You may feel confused at first, but it's important that you don't let this get in the way of your friendship. Listen and acknowledge how they feel. It may have taken a huge amount of courage to share this with you.

DO show your friend that you really care about them, and that you will support them.

DON'T dismiss their feelings as a phase. It's likely that your friend has thought long and hard about taking the big step of telling you or other people about this. And DON'T try to change or pressurise them. Let them explore their gender identity with you in a gentle open-ended way.

DISCUSS

1. Read Zayn's and Jess's stories. What do you learn from their different experiences?

2. Read what the school counsellor says. Do you agree? Explain your views.

RESEARCH

Research what kinds of support are available for young people questioning their gender identity. You could start with the Stonewall website, and also find out about the NHS Gender Identity Development Service.

3.1 Women's rights

In the UK, the battle for equal rights and treatment for women has been raging for over one hundred years.

Even though the law has changed in many ways, inequalities remain. Women are discriminated against in different ways throughout the world.

Women's rights in the UK – the successes

1878 The University of London allows women to take its degrees – the first university in the UK to do so.

1918 Some women over 30 are given the right to vote.

1920 Women are allowed to enter the legal and accountancy professions.

1925 The Law of Property Act allows husband and wife to inherit property equally.

1928 Women are given the same voting rights as men.

1958 Women are allowed to sit in the House of Lords.

1961 The contraceptive pill becomes available on the NHS.

1967 The Abortion Act gives women in the UK (excluding Northern Ireland) the right to have an abortion .

1970 The Equal Pay Act is passed as a direct result of the strike by women sewing machinists at Ford Dagenham.

1975 The Sex Discrimination Act outlaws discrimination by gender in workplaces and education.

1986 Statutory maternity pay is introduced.

1994 Rape within marriage is outlawed (before this a husband could not be charged with raping his wife).

2015 The first female bishop in the Church of England and first female senior officer in the British Army are appointed.

The challenges that remain

In 2016 the Fawcett Society reported these statistics:

- The pay gap now stands at 13.9 per cent for full-time work, and at the current rate of progress it will take 50 years to close the gender pay gap.

- Women make up 39 per cent of senior civil service roles, 14 per cent of police commissioners, 21 per cent of high court judges, and 12.7 per cent of officers in the armed forces. The UK ranks 39th in the world for representation of women in parliament.

- 107 104 cases of violence against women were prosecuted in 2014–15.

- Over 137 000 women in England and Wales are already living with the consequences of FGM (female genital mutilation). (See Unit 3.3.)

- Male graduates continue to earn more than female graduates even when compared with women who did the same subject, went to a similar university and went into the same industry.

- Women are far more likely to work part time (73 per cent of part-time employees are women).

- Women continue to play a greater role in caring for children and sick or older relatives. As a result, more women work part time. These jobs are typically lower paid with fewer opportunities for progression.

DISCUSS

1. Look at the timeline of women's rights in the UK. Which do you think is the most important milestone in the history of women's struggle for equal rights with men? Why?

2. Which of the challenges listed above shock you the most?

3. What demands or assumptions are made about women that are not made of men? Think about the workplace and at home.

4. Why do you think the cards are still stacked against women in the UK, even though they have won equal rights under the law?

RESEARCH

Research and write a paragraph describing each of the following in relation to your answer to question 1 about the timeline of women's rights:

a) what the situation was like for women before that date

b) the campaign to change the situation

c) why it was an important step for women's rights.

Malala's story

Malala Yousafzai grew up in an area of Pakistan that fell under the control of the Taliban. The Taliban tried to stop girls from going to school, denying them an education. Malala bravely spoke out against this in public and on her blog. As a result, the Taliban sent a gunman to shoot her.

She was shot in the head but luckily she survived. On her recovery, she continued her fight to defend the rights of girls to have access to a safe and high quality education. On her 16th birthday, she spoke at the United Nations and in 2014 she was awarded the Nobel Prize for Peace.

On her 21st birthday in 2018, she spoke in Brazil, where 1.5 million girls are currently denied an education.

DISCUSS

Read 'Malala's story'.

1. Why do you think Malala fights so hard for the rights of girls to be educated in Pakistan and around the world?

2. 'One child, one teacher, one book, one pen can change the world.' What does Malala mean?

3. What do you find most inspiring in Malala's story?

Women in sport

Although a lot of progress has been made in recent years, women and girls are far from equal with men in the world of sport. For example, the prize money for women's events is usually much less than for men's events.

There is much more media coverage of men's sports than women's sports, and among TV presenters the men far outnumber the women. Newspapers devote several pages to men's sports while women's sports get only a fraction of that space.

Progress has been made, but there is still a long way to go and sexist attitudes are still common.

RESEARCH

What changes need to be made to give women more equality in sport? Find out about the Women in Sport campaign and write a paragraph saying what you think needs to be done to change attitudes.

21

3.2 Violence against women

Women are the victims of violence every day, across all levels of society and in every country. This is true in the UK too, even though the legal battle for women's rights and gender equality may appear to have been won.

Sexism and hate crimes

At home, in public or at work, women frequently have to endure comments that are insulting or patronising. They may, more worryingly, be subjected to sexual harassment. Often they are expected to 'put up with' this sort of treatment. Women in this situation may sometimes feel, 'this is just the way things are', or they may fear being accused of overreacting by complaining. But such acts of casual sexism are dangerous as well as insulting for its victims. They normalise the power imbalance between men and women and make even more serious attacks on women more likely.

This is why some people, such as the MP Stella Creasy, are campaigning for misogyny (acts of prejudice against women) to be recognised as a hate crime, just as offences based on race, religion or sexual orientation are. It would mean that hate incidents would be recorded by the police, and judges could impose tougher sentences on the offender.

Here are some girls' and women's experiences:

'My male friends use words like "pussy" and "slut" to refer to girls all the time. When I complain they either laugh or give me a hard time. It makes me feel bad.' *Laura*

'The photos of celebrities in gossip magazines, with comments criticising their looks or their bodies, are usually of women. How many more body shaming pictures of women in bikinis have you seen, compared with those of men in trunks?' *Evie*

'My boss insists that I wear a dress and high heels at work "because it sells more". The men don't get the same treatment.' *Kim*

What is sexual harassment?

Sexual harassment is any unwanted behaviour of a sexual nature that makes you feel uncomfortable, scared or humiliated. It can be verbal, for example sexual comments, emails with sexual content, sexual jokes or photos. It can also include physical harassment, including unwanted kissing or touching.

Sexual harassment can happen anywhere, from the school corridor to the street to the workplace. It causes a lot of stress, and over time it can lead to physical and emotional problems, such as depression, anxiety and loss of self-confidence. Some people even feel forced to give up their jobs because of sexual harassment at work.

Sexual harassment at work is still so widespread that at the end of 2018 the government announced that it is introducing a new code of practice for employers to tackle the problem more effectively.

Under the Equality Act 2010, sexual harassment is a form of unlawful discrimination. If the harassment is physical, featuring any sort of sexual touching that the victim does not consent to, then the perpetrator could be charged with the offence of sexual assault under the Sexual Offences Act 2003.

DISCUSS

1. Why is sexual harassment a serious matter?

2. When a person is harassed in the street or workplace, they often don't feel they can respond, or report it. Why do you think this is?

3. What are good strategies for dealing with this kind of harassment?

Domestic abuse

Domestic violence or abuse refers to many types of abuse that occur in couple relationships or in families. It isn't just physical and sexual abuse, but includes emotional abuse, such as constant comments putting a person down. Controlling behaviour, such as stalking, checking a partner's texts or excessive jealousy, is also abusive. Coercive or controlling behaviour in an intimate or family relationship was made a criminal offence in England and Wales in 2015.

Approximately 2 million incidents of domestic abuse are reported each year in the UK, but the problem is bigger than this as many victims do not tell anyone about the abuse. The majority of the victims are female. On average, each year, two women a week are killed by a current or former male partner.

'It started with jealousy, checking my phone and emails, disapproving of male friends despite having female friends himself. [...] He once threw a hot bowl of soup at me, scalding me and smashing the bowl. He then grabbed the smashed crockery and slashed his wrist with it. I also had minor cuts on my wrist which he inflicted. Afterwards he denied what he had done to me [...] and it was all about his suicide attempt. I went back with him. A few years later I finally ended this abusive relationship after the birth of my second child. He was vile during that most emotional and vulnerable time. Enough was enough.' Michelle

Source: Safe Lives website

DISCUSS

1. What do you learn about domestic abuse from Michelle's story?

2. Why do you think it is often difficult for the victims of domestic violence to end or escape from the abuse? Think about:

   a) the control that occurs in the relationship

   b) what the victim loses when they challenge or leave their partner

   c) how dangerous it might be for women and children to leave an abusive relationship.

3.3 Forced marriage, honour-based violence and FGM

Some communities or societies seek to control women and their bodies in many different ways. Forced marriage, honour-based violence and female genital mutilation (FGM) are some of the most damaging – and illegal – practices that occur in the UK.

Forced marriages

A forced marriage is one where you face physical or emotional pressure to marry. You may be told that not marrying will bring shame on your family. Most forced marriages involving British citizens or residents take place overseas, with the victim being taken abroad for the ceremony.

Fact check

- Forced marriage is illegal in England and Wales. The legal age of marriage at which you can marry or form a civil partnership is 18 from 2023.

- The government's Forced Marriage Unit dealt with nearly 1200 cases in 2017 but believe that the actual number of cases is far higher.

- Forcing someone to marry can result in a sentence of up to 7 years in prison.

Forced marriages are not to be confused with arranged marriages (see page 49).

Nazanine's story

My parents said they wanted me to have an arranged marriage. I said yes, provided I had the final choice. I met several people they had selected but didn't like any of them.

With the last guy, they wouldn't let the issue go. My uncles have been pestering me, saying that I should marry him. Suddenly I'm told we're going on a holiday to Pakistan this summer. I've heard stories of forced marriages, with girls having their passports taken away by their families while abroad, until they agree to go through with the wedding. I don't know what to do.

Advice from the charity Karma Nirvana

If you are concerned that you will be forced into marriage when abroad, contact us (0800 5999 247, Mon–Fri). Once you leave the country, it is much harder to get help. However, there are some steps you can take to improve your situation when abroad. Take the address and contact details of a trusted friend and of the High Commission/Embassy in the country you are visiting. You should also take some money, both in sterling and in the local currency, along with a spare mobile phone. Photocopy your passport and tickets before you leave.

RESEARCH

Using the internet, research the problem of forced marriages, and what other advice and support is available to girls in situations like Nazanine's. You could look up the charities Karma Nirvana or The Halo Project or search for 'forced marriage' in the Gov.uk website.

I DON'T

You can't force love

Don't force marriage

If you or someone you know is being forced into a marriage contact:

Karma Nirvana Helpline:

Honour-based abuse

Forced marriage is one aspect of a wider practice which has been given the name 'honour-based abuse' or 'honour-based violence'.

The idea of 'honour' is very important in some communities and cultures. If someone does something to bring dishonour or shame on the family or community, they can be severely punished. Punishment can be through emotional abuse, physical abuse, family disownment and, in some cases, even murder. This punishment can be carried out by the immediate family, the extended family, and/or the wider community.

Although women are often the victims of honour-based crimes, this is not always the case. Women can also be perpetrators.

There are on average 12 to 15 honour killings in the UK each year, according to the charity Halo Project.

DISCUSS

Discuss what Sunanda means. Do you agree?

'There is no "honour" in honour-based violence. Let's call it what it is – a human rights abuse. Using the term "honour" gives criminals an excuse to hide behind for their crimes.' **Sunanda**

Female genital mutilation (FGM)

FGM, also known as female circumcision, is the surgical removal or mutilation of a girl's or a woman's genitalia for non-medical reasons. It is practised by certain communities in parts of Africa, the Middle East and Asia, even though it is now illegal in most countries. Some people in the societies that practise it say it is an important and traditional part of their culture often linked to preserving a girl's virginity or preparing her for adulthood and marriage. In fact, it is a means of controlling women's bodies and their sexuality. The World Health Organization has called FGM a violation of the human rights of women and girls.

FGM can damage a girl's or woman's health in many ways. In the short term, lack of hygiene can result in severe infections including tetanus. There can be damage to the wider genital area, and the person can die from blood loss from the cutting. In the longer term, women experience difficulties in menstruation, urinating, giving birth, and in having and enjoying sex. The procedure and its effects can be psychologically traumatic.

Female genital mutilation is a problem in the UK, as there are many communities from Eritrea, Ethiopia, Nigeria and Somalia where FGM is practised. Girls are often taken to their or their family's country of origin to be cut, even though this has been illegal since 2003.

Fact check

- According to the campaigning group Forward, 60 000 girls under 15 are at risk of FGM in the UK, and 137 000 girls and women are living with the consequences of FGM.

- The Female Genital Mutilation Act 2003 makes it illegal to practise FGM in England and Wales. It is also illegal to take girls who are British nationals or permanent residents of the UK abroad for FGM, whether or not it is lawful in that country. It is also illegal to fail to protect a person from FGM if you are responsible for them.

- The first successful prosecution for FGM in the UK was in 2019.

RESEARCH

1. Find out more about FGM by going on the World Health Organization website and searching for 'female genital mutilation'.

    a) What reasons are given for why is it practised in some countries?

    b) What are the long-term effects of FGM?

    c) How are countries and international agencies working to end the practice?

    d) What support is offered to victims or those threatened by FGM? Research one of the organisations listed on the Womankind website.

2. Use the BBC News website to find out what the practice of breast ironing involves. Do you think this should be made a specific offence in UK law, in the same way that FGM is?

3.4 LGBTQ+ rights

The lesbian, gay, bi, trans and queer (LGBTQ+) communities in the UK have worked hard to secure equal rights.

LGBTQ+ citizens in the UK now have most of the same legal rights as non-LGBTQ+ citizens. However, the situation is very different in other countries.

Fact check

A timeline of LGBTQ+ rights in the UK

1967 Sex between men over 21 years old becomes legal in England and Wales (1980 in Scotland; 1982 in Northern Ireland).

1984 Chris Smith becomes the first openly gay MP in the United Kingdom.

2000 Gay people are permitted to join the armed forces.

2001 The age of consent for sex between men is lowered from 18 to 16.

2004 Same-sex couples are granted civil partnerships as an equivalent to marriage.

2004 The right is granted for transgender people to change their gender legally, for example to get a new birth certificate.

2002 Gay and lesbian single persons and same-sex couples are granted the right to adopt a child.

2013 Nikki Sinclaire is the first openly trans UK Member of the European Parliament (MEP).

2014 Same-sex couples are granted the right to marry.

RESEARCH

Research one of the events in the timeline. How did it improve the lives of LGBT+ people?

LGBTQ+ rights under the law in the UK

The Equality Act 2010 prohibits schools, shops, hotels and other providers of goods and services from discriminating on the grounds of sexual orientation or gender reassignment.

Respecting gender identity at school, for example, means using people's preferred pronouns, and allowing students to use gender neutral toilets or toilets of the gender they identify with.

The same Act also protects LGBTQ+ people from discrimination and harassment at work. This applies to work experience students and temporary workers as much as to full-time workers. So LGBTQ+ people cannot be paid less money than or be given different benefits from others.

Harassment includes jokes and 'banter', not just insults and threats. If an employee feels they are being targeted because of their sexual orientation or gender identity, and they feel offended, then the behaviour counts as harassment and is unlawful.

Homophobic, biphobic and transphobic bullying

Homophobic and biphobic bullying is bullying aimed at lesbian, gay and bisexual people. It often involves homophobic language, which includes using words like 'gay' or 'lesbian' in a negative way. Picking on gay classmates or colleagues or pestering them with intrusive questions is also bullying.

Transphobic bullying is using similar language and behaviour to target trans people, for example referring to someone as a 'tranny' or not using their preferred pronouns.

Both kinds of bullying are unacceptable and cause huge distress to its victims. Yet they are also very common. A survey by Cambridge University in 2017 found that 45 per cent of LGBT+ students are bullied for being LGBT+ at school.

Four teenagers explain what homophobia and transphobia means to them.

Being singled out
'I get pointed at in the corridor, and my friends get laughed at for hanging around with me.' Matt

Being abused
'It went from insults to actual attacks. I was afraid of going home on my own.' Meghan

Having to keep relationships secret
'I can't walk out openly with my girlfriend because our families wouldn't approve of us going out together.' Gemma

Being on the end of ignorance
'My parents talk about being bi as "just a phase", as something I will grow out of.' Seamus

DISCUSS

Read 'How to deal with bullying'.

1. What effects do homophobia or transphobia have on young people?

2. Why do you think some people are homophobic or transphobic?

3. What does your school do to prevent homophobic and transphobic bullying?

How to deal with bullying

As with any bullying, it is always useful to keep a written record of all the incidents. However small they seem in themselves, they may add up to a significant body of evidence if and when you need to take it further. Remember that it is illegal to be treated in this way.

Tell an adult you trust. They will act to protect your rights.

Challenge such insults clearly and calmly, as long as you feel safe and confident to do so. For example, ask a question like, 'How would you feel if someone spoke to you in that way?' Or say how you feel: 'I'm surprised that you are using "gay" as a term of abuse.' Or confront it directly: 'That is offensive.'

LGBT+ rights abroad

LGBT+ rights in the UK have been hard won over the last 50 years, though the battle to end discrimination continues. However, there are over 50 countries in the world where sex between people of the same gender is illegal, including nearly two-thirds of Commonwealth countries. In some countries, homosexuality carries the death penalty. Even in countries where it is legal, there is very little protection for gay rights, and being openly bi, gay or trans requires a lot of courage.

The Olympic diver Tom Daley spoke out at the 2018 Commonwealth Games to condemn anti-gay laws in 37 of the competing Commonwealth countries.

YOUR CHOICE

Think about the two statements below. Discuss what you think are the best things that people can do to advance LGBT+ rights and end discrimination.

'Now that LGBT+ rights have been won in the UK, we have to put pressure on other countries in the world to repeal their anti-gay laws.'

'Passing laws is all well and good, but we still get picked on and treated differently. You need to change people's attitudes instead.'

RESEARCH

Choose one of these countries: Russia, United Arab Emirates, Jamaica, Nigeria.

Find out:

1. what rights, if any, LGBT+ people have

2. to what extent LGBT+ people are persecuted there.

4.1 Racism in education and at work

Racism is the belief that some ethnic groups are better than others. This attitude is shown through acts of violence, aggression or discrimination towards people of a different ethnicity.

Educational racism

Racial discrimination is when a person or particular group of people are treated differently or worse because of their skin colour, nationality, ethnicity or religion. Sometimes discrimination is overt, for example when minority ethnic students face bullying, intimidation and violence at school. At other times, discrimination can be covert, which is not so obvious. This might be, for example, when a particular group of students are discriminated against through school applications, during lessons or while applying to university.

DISCUSS

Look at the situations listed below. Answer the questions and give reasons for your views.

a) A White girl is told than she cannot join in a skipping game with a group of Black girls, because it was 'their game'.

b) A group of White boys pick on a Black boy at school, calling him unpleasant names.

c) A Hindu girl is told she cannot have the day off to celebrate Diwali, the festival of light. Previously, Muslim students in the same school had the day off to celebrate the end of Ramadan.

d) A Jewish student wants to bring kosher food into school, and reheat it using a school microwave. The school says it does not provide this facility.

e) During a class discussion, a student is told that it's unfair that his dad has come to the UK from Poland to take British people's jobs.

1. Which do you think are dicriminatory?

2. Look at the examples you have chosen. Do they show covert or overt racial discrimination?

Banning religious symbols

At the beginning of term in 2013, Birmingham Metropolitan College tried to ban the niqab. This is a veil, worn by some Muslim girls and women, that covers the face apart from the eyes. The college Principal argued that the ban was necessary for security reasons, and that students' faces had to be seen in order for them to be identified. Muslim groups said that this was racist and discriminatory, singling out a particular religious group, mainly made up of Black, Arabic and South Asian students. They argued instead that when entering the college, students should be able to show their faces privately to a female security guard.

Over 8000 people signed a petition against the policy and the college accepted that the policy could not continue. Students are now allowed to wear the niqab at college.

DISCUSS

Do you think the college was right to try to ban an item of clothing which some Muslim students choose to wear? Give reasons for your views.

RESEARCH

In France, it is illegal to wear any sign of your faith in school, whether this is a headscarf, a turban, a skullcap or a cross.

1. Research why the French government thought it was a good idea to ban all religious symbols in French schools. What do you think the advantages and disadvantages are of this?

2. Write two or three paragraphs on whether you think this decision is correct and compatible with human rights (see *Your Choice Book Two*, Unit 15.2). Give reasons for your views.

Employment racism

It is illegal to discriminate against a person at work on a wide range of grounds, including race. This includes hiring or not hiring somebody, giving or refusing a pay rise or promotion, and firing or keeping somebody simply on the grounds of their ethnicity.

In March 2018, a business psychology company carried out a survey of 1400 people, and 52 per cent said they had witnessed an act of racism at work. However, less than 20 per cent of them had reported this to their employer, who are legally responsible for monitoring racist incidents, intervening and solving them.

Of the people who did not report the incident, 40 per cent said it was because they were worried about the consequences. In other words, they were afraid that it would have a negative impact on their job if they spoke up.

The survey found Black people were the most likely to be discriminated against, at 69 per cent. The figure for Asian people was 54 per cent and for White people was 45 per cent.

Fact check

The Equality Act 2010 legally protects people in the UK from discrimination in the workplace and in wider society.

It states that it is against the law to discriminate against anyone because of age, gender reassignment, being married or in a civil partnership, being pregnant or on maternity leave, disability, race including colour, nationality, ethnic or national origin, religion or belief, sex and sexual orientation.

It protects people from discrimination at work, in education, as a consumer, when using public services and when buying or renting property.

RESEARCH

Research what laws there are against racial discrimination at work according to ACAS, what offences you can be tried for and what the punishments for these offences are. Write a summary of two or three paragraphs.

DISCUSS

Imagine that you are responsible for monitoring and reducing racism in a company.

1. What policies and procedures would you have for dealing with racism and racial discrimination?
2. What punishments and sanctions would you have for racist behaviour?
3. Would you have any rewards for promoting inclusion in the workplace?
4. What training could be included to increase inclusivity?

   Give reasons for your views.

Racism in sport: Kick It Out

Kick It Out started in 1993 to combat racism in football. It began as a small charity, but is now funded by the Premier League, the Football League, the Football Association and the Professional Footballer's Association.

In 2015–16, Kick It Out received 469 reports of abuse, compared with 402 in the previous year. Of these, 48 per cent were related to race and racial discrimination, 21 per cent related to homophobic, biphobic and transphobic incidents, and 17 per cent were faith related.

Racial abuse reported to Kick It Out included:

- the singing of racist songs at football matches
- name-calling and bullying of minority ethnic players at football matches
- racist abuse and bullying of ethnic minority fans travelling to or at football matches
- racist abuse on social media.

In spite of the campaign, racism continues at football matches in the UK and abroad. IIn 2021, England players Marcus Rashford, Jadon Sancho and Bukayo Saka received a torrent of racial abuse online after missing penalties in the Euro 2020 final against Italy. 12 people were arrested in the UK and one man received a jail sentence for his part in the abuse.

WRITE

You are a club manager. You want to make sure there is no racism at a local football game. Create a poster to be displayed at the game, to encourage good behaviour and discourage racism.

4.2 Racism and society

Racism can be shown through negativity, aggression, discrimination, bias or prejudice towards someone of a particular ethnicity.

It is against the law to discriminate against people on a wide range of grounds, including age, sex, gender reassignment, sexual orientation, race, religion and ethnicity. By law, public institutions such as schools must have equal opportunity policies and abide by the Equality Act (2010) to make sure that nobody is discriminated against.

Discrimination, which is about action, is different from prejudice, which is about our thoughts. Prejudice means having unfair feelings, opinions or attitudes to others, especially when they are different in some way to yourself.

Nigel Farage, UKIP leader during the 2016 EU referendum campaign, stands in front of a UKIP poster showing a queue of migrants and refugees. His opponents say it was racist; he says it was just about immigration. What do you think?

RESEARCH

Look at a copy of your school's equal opportunities policy. What groups are listed? Is there anything else you think should be added?

Racism and xenophobia

Racism can include a fear or hatred of people of a different ethnicity. This is different from xenophobia, which is a fear or hatred of foreigners. So, a White supremacist racist will dislike all Black or Asian people – whether or not they were born in the UK. By contrast, a xenophobe will dislike foreigners.

In the past, there have been racist parties in the UK. The British National Party (BNP) had the racist policy of wanting to take UK citizenship away from non-white citizens.

In the years leading up to the EU referendum in 2016, critics of UKIP – the United Kingdom Independence Party – argued that it is racist. (UKIP was founded in 1993 to campaign for Britain to leave the European Union.) However, UKIP denied that it was racist, saying it had no problem with the people of Europe. Instead, UKIP has said it is the institution of the European Union, and uncontrolled immigration, that it dislikes.

DISCUSS

1. Look at the image above and the two quotations below about UKIP, and read a news article about UKIP chosen by your teacher.

   Do you think UKIP was racist or xenophobic? And does this distinction matter? Give reasons for your views.

   - 'UKIP has done more to defeat the BNP than any other political party.' Nigel Farage, former leader of UKIP

   - 'UKIP is deliberately whipping up fear and – by extension – hatred of foreigners with its provocative posters and inflammatory language.' Nick Lowles, Director of HOPE not Hate

2. UK Home Office figures showed a steep increase in the number of recorded hate crimes in the month following the EU referendum in June 2016. Why do you think this might be?

No platform versus freedom of speech

Some universities have banned racist speakers, saying there is no place for them on campus. This is known as a 'no platform' policy. Others argue that the best way to defeat racism is by engaging racist speakers and then defeating them with rational argument and debate.

DISCUSS

What do you think are the pros and cons of 'no platforming' speakers? Come up with three reasons in favour and three against and then explain your own views.

Institutional racism and the police

Institutional racism is when racism and racist behaviour are seen as normal within an organisation. The problem is not new. The term became widely known more than two decades ago through the Macpherson Report in 1999. This report uncovered wide institutional racism in the police following the 1993 murder of Stephen Lawrence, a Black teenager, in London and the subsequent botched investigation of the crime. Five people were initially arrested but no one was convicted. Eighteen years later, there was another trial and two people were finally convicted of the murder.

Institutional racism still plagues policing, warns chief constable

Chief Constable Gareth Wilson, the lead on diversity for the National Police Chiefs Council (NPCC), told the Guardian police forces had been too slow to eliminate prejudice from the workforce and change the way officers treat the communities they serve.

Under new plans unveiled by the NPCC, performance reviews of top officers will be tied to their success in improving diversity. [...]

The diversity plan was announced as fresh figures showed police forces are much whiter than the populations they serve. This is despite promises made almost two decades ago after the Macpherson report into the failings that allowed the racist killers of the black schoolboy Stephen Lawrence escape justice.

Wilson said the police had made progress but that change had been too slow, and that the measures would help make forces look more like Britain. [...]

Official figures show that racial disparity is now worse for stop and search. According to government figures, between 2010–11 and 2014–15, the likelihood of black people being searched fell from six times that of white people to four times. But in 2016–17 that [...] rose again: black people were eight times more likely than white people to be stopped by police, with the vast majority [of searches] producing no evidence of involvement in crime.

The latest figures show that 7% of police officers are from a black and minority ethnic (BAME) background, compared with 14% of the population as a whole. [...] Nowhere is that gap worse than in the Metropolitan police. London's 40% BAME population is policed by a 14% BAME police force.

Wilson said staff support associations for black, disabled and LGBT officers are sceptical about whether the new plans will work. 'There is great concern among support staff networks that nothing will change,' he said.

From *The Guardian*, 12 October 2018

DISCUSS

Stop and search means that a police officer can stop and search you if they have a good reason to suspect that you're carrying illegal drugs, a weapon, stolen property or something which could be used to commit a crime, such as a crowbar.

1. What do you think 'racial disparity' means in relation to stop and search?

2. Do you think there would be less racial disparity in stop and search if there were more police officers from ethnic minority backgrounds?

RESEARCH

Use the internet to investigate the murder of Stephen Lawrence, and the institutional racism that the Macpherson Report uncovered over two decades ago. Write two or three paragraphs about what happened.

5.1 Safety at parties

Parties are fun but sometimes things can go wrong. It is important that you know how to keep yourself safe at parties.

Fact check

Remember: if you are under 18 it is illegal

- for you to buy alcohol
- for an adult to buy you alcohol*
- for anyone to sell you alcohol.

* If you are 16 or 17 and with an adult in a pub or restaurant you can be bought beer, wine or cider to drink with a meal.

Before the party: plan ahead

- Know where you are going and how you are going to get there. It may seem obvious, but you don't want to get stranded somewhere and not know where you are going.
- Always tell a trusted adult where you will be.
- Arrange a password with a trusted adult or friend. When you use this (for example, by text) they will know to remove you from the situation.
- If there's a chance you may have sexual contact with someone, take some condoms or dental dams with you. It's better to be prepared.
- Think through how to avoid any peer pressure to buy or drink alcohol.
- If you are planning to drink alcohol, have something to eat before you go out. However, remember that eating before drinking alcohol does NOT make drinking safe.
- Plan how you are going to get home. Take enough money for a taxi if you might need one and have a few reputable taxi numbers with you.

At the party

- Don't be pressurised into doing something you don't want to. Say 'no' firmly.

- If you feel you must drink alcohol, set yourself a limit and stick to it. Have a non-alcoholic drink after each alcoholic one, alternating between the two.
- Keep an eye on your drink. Never leave it unattended because someone could spike it.
- Don't take illegal drugs. And don't mix drugs and alcohol, even prescribed drugs like antibiotics. They make a lethal combination.
- Stick with your friends. Don't get separated from them. There's safety in numbers.
- Trust your instincts. If they tell you that a situation isn't safe, then the chances are it isn't.
- If you feel the situation is getting out of hand, for example if there's a fight, leave the party and go somewhere safe.
- Think carefully about which selfies you post and whether posting pictures of others would cause upset or harm.

After the party

- Stick to your plan. Don't be tempted to miss your lift or bus because you are having such a good time. If you can, head home together; there is safety in numbers.
- Never accept a lift from a stranger and don't get into a car that's being driven by someone who has been drinking or taking drugs.
- If you are walking home, stick to streets that are well lit and walk with somebody rather than on your own.
- Don't take shortcuts down dark alleyways. Go the long way round even though it takes more time.
- If for any reason your lift doesn't turn up, share a taxi with someone else. If you can't find a taxi, phone one or get someone to call one for you.

YOUR CHOICE

Which are the most useful pieces of advice given above? On your own, pick out what you think is the most useful advice for what to do before a party, at a party and after a party. Then share your opinions in a group.

WRITE

Based on what you have read above, list five bullet points highlighting the dangers that can occur at parties.

Spiking drinks and needle spiking

Spiking drinks is when someone puts alcohol or drugs into your drink without you knowing, when you are not looking. Needle spiking is when someone injects someone else with drugs without their consent. Spiking someone's drink or needle spiking can make them seriously ill or even kill them. If their drink is spiked with a drug like GHB they may do something they wouldn't normally do (such as have sex) and be unable to remember doing it. To spike someone's drink, even as a prank, is a crime.

Fact check

Spiking is a criminal offence for which a maximum sentence is ten years in prison. If the offence is linked to a rape or sexual assault the sentence can be longer.

According to the National Police Chief's Council, there were 2581 reports of spiking by needle and 2131 reports of drink spiking between 2021 and 2022.

A survey of 2000 women (by the ITV show *This Morning*) revealed that:

- 1 in 5 believed they had had their drinks spiked on a night out.
- 1 in 3 admitted to leaving their drinks unattended.
- 82 per cent of those who thought that their drinks had been spiked did not report it.

RESEARCH

1. What advice do the police give for people to protect themselves?
2. What advice does the NHS give on drink spiking?

Lucy's story

It was a right laugh. It was Toby's idea. There's this girl called Jasmine in our year who doesn't drink alcohol and always drinks some fancy non-alcoholic drink. Toby said he'd slip some alcohol into her drink, so I distracted her while he spiked her drink. She didn't seem to notice, but when she got up to dance she was staggering all over the place. It was so funny that I videoed her. Then I shared it online. At school on Monday everyone was watching it. It was hilarious.

DISCUSS

1. What do you think of the way Toby and Lucy behaved?
2. How do you think Jasmine felt?
3. How might Jasmine have been in danger from having her drink spiked?
4. Should she report the incident to the police?
5. What would be the consequences of **a)** reporting it and **b)** not reporting it?
6. How could you make sure that Toby and Lucy never behave like that in the future?

If things go wrong

If something happens at a party that you are upset or worried about, talk to a family member or an adult whom you trust.

You may be concerned that you will get into trouble either with your parents/carers or the police. Perhaps you weren't where you said you would be, or you did something silly. You must weigh up the consequences of speaking about it or staying silent, and then do the right thing. Always put safety first.

Top tips on how to protect yourself

- Never leave your drink unattended. If you go to the toilet, get a friend to watch it for you.
- Only drink drinks bought by people you trust.
- Be careful not to get too close to strangers in a club, bar or party and stay alert to what they might be doing.
- If you feel a pinprick and think that you've been needle spiked, seek immediate medical attention.

5.2 Your online reputation

Your reputation is what people say about you when you are not there. Are you a reliable person? Do you like to have a joke? Are you trustworthy?

Your online reputation is also what people think about you, but it is based purely on what they see about you and your activities online. Because of this you should be careful about:

- becoming obsessed with your online reputation
- creating a false impression of yourself
- getting a false impression of other people
- attacking other people to make yourself feel better.

It is also very important to realise that your online reputation will follow you into adulthood, so images, tweets and posts that you share now can reflect badly on you in later life.

Online obsession

Many people are concerned with the way they look or sound online, or with how popular they are. The problem is when people get obsessed with their online image, how many likes they get on Facebook or Twitter, or how good they look on Snapchat or Instagram, and it affects their lives negatively.

Brian's story

It started out as a friendly competition with a few mates who I went to the gym with. We were all trying to get the perfect set of photos of us working out. At first it was just a joke, but gradually I got more and more obsessed with taking the perfect selfie. I began taking more and more photos. Eventually, it got to over 100 photos per day.

I started dieting to make myself look better. I was obsessed with getting the perfect boy-band photo. I stopped eating and started lying to my parents about it.

My parents started to realise that something was wrong and eventually manged to convince me to go to the doctor. I'm starting to accept that I have a problem and to understand my condition, but I'm still battling with anorexia.

Stacey's story

I was the most popular girl in my year at my old school. But then my parents changed jobs and we moved to a different city, so I lost all my friends and had to start over.

At the new school, it was difficult to make friends, so I went online to talk to people. At first it was just with my old friends to see how they were doing, but gradually it became more important. I wanted to get as many likes as possible. I would do anything, say anything and share anything just to get more likes. It didn't matter if the likes were from friends or strangers. All I wanted was to be popular.

One day my dad asked to see me. He was really upset. He pointed out some of the posts I had been sharing. It turned out they were from Britain First – a really nasty racist online group. I hadn't been reading the posts – just sharing them as they seemed to be popular and I wanted to get more likes. We sat down and had a talk about things, and I realised that what I was doing online was not making me happy or less lonely. Now I'm much more careful about what I share online and I am spending more time making friends in the real world.

Gemma's story

When I was 14, I was online and started chatting to this boy, Sam, who I really liked. We became good friends and used to chat with each other once a week. Then once a week turned to twice a week, and then pretty much every day.

Sam looked really cute in his photo, and I gradually found myself developing feelings for him. I was delighted when I found out he felt the same way. Yet whenever I talked about meeting up, he dodged the question, even though he only lived half an hour away from me.

It was after about a year and a half that I saw another photo of Sam – but it was a minor celebrity from a boy band whose name wasn't Sam! I had been lied to. I confronted Sam online, and he finally agreed to meet up.

When he turned up, it was a boy from my school who said he fancied me and wanted to get to know me. I had been catfished, which I found out means somebody pretends to be somebody else to get to know you romantically. I was gutted. If he had lied to me about who he was, how could I ever trust him?

Now if I want to get closer to somebody I've met online, I insist on meeting them – face-to-face, in a public place – and I take a friend or tell somebody where I'm going.

DISCUSS

1. What do you think the problem was in each of the cases above?

2. What could each person have done differently?

3. What would you do if you or a friend were confronted with such behaviour online?

Give reasons for your views.

YOUR CHOICE

In pairs, read the statements below.

- Rank them in order from the most important to the least important.

- Then compare your answers with another pair.

Give reasons for your views.

1. Making sure you don't share offensive material online.

2. Having an attractive profile picture of yourself on social media.

3. Getting lots of likes for your posts.

4. Posting only occasionally online, because it's about quality, not quantity.

5. Posting every day, to show people that you are up to date with the latest news.

6. Supporting friends online if they are attacked by trolls.

7. Ignoring trolls when they attack you or your friends online.

8. Having a short description of yourself that accurately reflects who you are and what you believe in but doesn't give away too much personal information (for example, where you live or go to school) so people can't identify you.

9. Sharing photos of yourself regularly so everyone can see what you've been up to.

10. Always responding to somebody online when you disagree with them, because it's right that you should stick up for your views.

6.1 Heroin and cocaine

All legal and illegal drugs carry risks, but some are more dangerous than others. Two of the most dangerous illegal drugs are heroin and cocaine, because of their effects.

Heroin

Heroin is a class A drug made from the seeds of the opium poppy. It is used in hospitals as a very powerful painkiller.

What are the effects of heroin?

Heroin users get a pleasurable sensation known as a 'rush' – a feeling of wellbeing. Depending on the size of the dose the user may feel sleepy and very relaxed.

What are the risks of taking heroin?

Heroin is very addictive. The first time you take heroin can lead to an addiction in the long term. A user quickly develops tolerance and needs larger and more frequent fixes to get the same effect. Once someone is addicted, their body will respond badly if they don't take the drug regularly, and they will get withdrawal symptoms, which can be very serious.

There are other serious risks to taking heroin:

- If the heroin is injected, it can damage veins and arteries.
- There is a risk of contracting infections such as hepatitis and HIV from sharing needles and syringes.
- There is the risk of overdosing, especially if the heroin is taken with other drugs or alcohol.
- Because heroin is such a strong sedative and stops a user from coughing properly, if someone is sick while they are asleep, they can choke on their own vomit.

Heroin can ruin people's lives. They crave the next fix so much that they may turn to crime, even stealing from their family and friends, to get the money to pay for the drug. It can cost as much as £100 a day for an addict to buy the heroin they crave. Their relationships suffer and they may lose their jobs and their homes.

Heroin bought on the street is often mixed with other substances such as sugar, powdered milk and starch.

Cocaine

Cocaine is a class A drug that acts as a stimulant, speeding up the way your mind and body work. It comes as a white powder which can be snorted or smoked, or in small lumps as crack cocaine which can be smoked. Cocaine can also be injected.

What are the effects of cocaine?

Cocaine makes users feel wide awake and full of confidence, and can make people reckless. Smoking crack cocaine has an almost immediate effect, but it only lasts for about ten minutes. Snorting cocaine takes longer to produce an effect, but this only lasts for about twenty minutes.

What are the risks of taking cocaine?

- Using cocaine can affect a person's mental health, making them depressed and run down.
- Cocaine is very addictive. Frequent users find that they want it more and more.
- People who snort cocaine regularly can damage, or completely destroy, the cartilage in their nose between their nostrils.

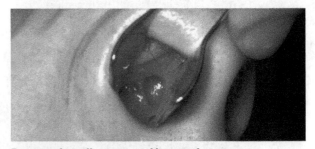

Damaged cartilage caused by cocaine use

- Taking too much cocaine can cause a number of health problems. Even young people who are otherwise healthy can suffer a fit or a heart attack.

- Cocaine is dangerous when taken with other drugs, particularly alcohol. When cocaine and alcohol are mixed, they produce a toxic chemical in the body.

Fact check

According to Public Health England, a heroin or crack cocaine addict is estimated to cost the country an average of £26000 a year in crime.

The cost to the NHS of treating people for drug misuse is £488 million a year.

In Switzerland, 'heroin-assisted treatment', which involves prescribing heroin to addicts in clinics, has cut the number of burglaries each year by half.

Treating drug abuse as a health problem has also reduced the amount of money made by the criminals who supply illegal drugs.

DISCUSS

1. Should addicts be able to get heroin or cocaine on prescription?

2. What would be the advantages and disadvantages of introducing such a system in the UK?

3. Would it help an addict to manage their addiction, or would it create more addicts who will face withdrawal symptoms when they miss their drugs?

WRITE

You are on the committee of a pressure group arguing for drugs such as heroin and cocaine to be available on prescription. Produce a petition to send to your MP. What statement will you be asking people to sign up and support?

My older sister is a heroin addict. How can I help her?

Having a heroin addict in the family affects the whole family. Here, Denise Lancaster offers some advice.

Stay strong. Don't be tempted to do things that will enable her to get out of situations that she finds herself in because of her habit. For example, don't lie for her when she asks you not to tell your parents.

Don't give in to any pressure from her to take drugs yourself.

Don't expect to be able to reason with her about quitting. The physical urge she has to take drugs because of her addiction is much too strong for you to be able to talk her out of it.

Talk to your doctor. It may be possible for her to get treatment on the NHS, if she gives her consent.

Don't expect to see results immediately. Coming off drugs can be a long and painful process.

Do offer support and try not to be judgemental.

Ask Erica

Dear Erica

My brother has recently starting messing about with drugs. He thinks it's cool and does it to show off in front of his mates. He says it makes him feel good. I'm not sure who to tell or what to do. What can I do?

Maxine

WRITE

Draft Erica's reply to Maxine.

TRUE OR FALSE

Do this test-yourself quiz about heroin. Which statements are true and which are false?

1. You will instantly become addicted the first time you take heroin.

2. Heroin is not an expensive drug.

3. The heroin sold on the streets is usually very pure.

4. Sharing needles is more risky than smoking or snorting heroin.

5. A heroin user will get withdrawal symptoms if they do not get their regular fix.

WRITE

In pairs, use the information about cocaine on this page and other information you can find on the internet to produce a test-yourself quiz on cocaine. Then give your quiz to another pair to do.

6.2 The impact of drugs

How should schools deal with drug incidents? What about incidents that occur near the school but not on school property?

A firm stand

Trevor Wilson is a parent and school governor. He is determined to make sure there is no drugs problem at his son's school. Recently there have been incidents of students going into town and smoking cannabis in the lunch hour and of a student being found in possession of unidentified tablets on the school premises. Mr Wilson feels that the school has not dealt with the incidents firmly enough. He is planning to raise the matter at the next parent-teacher's committee meeting. He wants the new school policy on drugs to make it quite clear that the school will not tolerate drugs in any way.

The school counsellor has a slightly different point of view, saying, 'Anyone who is dealing drugs at school should be expelled. But the punishment for other drug incidents at school should aim to help the person who is involved as well as to protect the other students.'

DISCUSS

1. Discuss Mr Wilson's point of view.

   a) Should schools have a zero-tolerance policy towards drugs and drug taking?

   b) Do you think Mr Wilson would have a different view if his son was one of the students who had been smoking cannabis in the lunch hour?

2. Discuss the school counsellor's view. Do you think it is too lenient, or do you think it is better than having a zero-tolerance policy?

RESEARCH

Find out what your school's drug policy is towards drug-related incidents such as the following:

- a student is suspected of having taken a drug and is under the influence of the drug

- an illegal drug is found on the school premises

- a student is caught using an illegal drug on the school premises

- a student is suspected of supplying drugs at the school gate

- an individual reveals that he has been taking drugs outside school and asks for help.

Drugs on the street

Organised gangs of criminals known as 'county lines' are targeting vulnerable young people and luring them into selling heroin and crack cocaine in towns across Britain. They are known as county lines because the gangs operate across county boundaries, using secure telephone lines to control the sale of drugs.

The gangs are based in cities such as Manchester and Birmingham and use children as runners to transport and sell drugs in rural areas such as Cumbria and Norfolk. This is known as 'going cunch' (country) or 'going OT' (out there).

The Children's Commissioner, Anne Longfield, interviewed in the *Daily Mail* in September 2018, said that: 'The grooming of children by gangs in county lines is a child protection crisis that needs attention at a national level to prevent children getting involved, to protect them and help them re-enter mainstream school and society.'

'Very often part of the process will arrange for that child on their first run to be robbed by someone in the gang and the child will come back and probably get beaten up and told now you owe us for the price of the drugs and the phone.'

Another way the gangs recruit young people is by targeting teenagers who smoke cannabis. Many of them do not have enough money to pay for the drug, so the gang leaders let them have it on a buy-now-pay-later basis. Gradually they build up the debt they owe the gang leaders, who tell them they can reduce the debt by working for them. If they try to refuse, they are threatened with violence.

Gang members identify people they can groom with promises of cash for travelling to make a delivery. To young teenagers it can seem a quick and easy way to make money. But once they are in, they are treated very differently.

Fact check

The number of children being enslaved as drug runners in towns across the country may be as high as 50 000, according to an estimate by Children's Commissioner Anne Longfield in 2018.

According to the Home Office, White British children aged 15 to 16 are most at risk of exploitation.

The National Crime Agency estimated that there were more than 1500 county lines selling Class A drugs in Britain.

Imagine you have a friend who has been asked to move a small amount of cannabis to another town where their cousins live the next time they visit. They have been offered a small amount of cash in return.

1. What dangers do you think they might face in such a situation?

2. What advice would you give your friend to persuade them not to get involved?

Give reasons for your views.

Portugal takes a different approach

In 2001, Portugal introduced a law which decriminalised the possession and the use of small quantities of all illegal drugs. Since then, if a person in Portugal is found in possession of a drug they may receive a small fine and be referred to a treatment centre. The matter is regarded as a health issue rather than a criminal one and the policy is supported by a very strong treatment programme for those with addictions.

What effect has the decriminalisation had on drug use? According to recent statistics, the number of cases of overdoses in Portugal has gone down. So has the number of drug-related HIV infections. There has also been a reduction in drug-related crime. Critics of the policy argue that statistics show personal drug use has risen since decriminalisation was introduced.

What are the arguments for and against the UK following Portugal's example and decriminalising the personal use of illegal drugs?

Work in groups. Draw a line down the middle of a large sheet of paper. On one side list the arguments for decriminalisation, and on the other list the arguments against. Then organise a debate on the issue.

7.1 Pregnancy

In 2016, 14.5 births per 1000 were to teenage parents. Pregnancy is the responsibility of both girls and boys.

How does pregnancy happen?

To become pregnant, semen (containing sperm) has to come into direct contact with an egg. This can happen through vaginal sex or through a fertility treatment such as IVF, and occasionally by sperm coming into contact with a girl's or woman's vagina.

You are most likely to become pregnant around the time of ovulation. This is when an egg is released from one of the ovaries and travels down the fallopian tube to the womb. Ovulation usually occurs about 14 days after the first day of a girl's period, but some girls have shorter cycles so it can be earlier.

Although the egg only lives for about 24 hours, sperm can survive inside a woman's body for up to seven days. The 'fertile window' can therefore be up to 8 days long.

How can you tell if you are pregnant?

The only way to know for sure if you are pregnant is to take a pregnancy test. This is available from any chemist. There are several symptoms to look out for, such as missing your period or having much lighter periods than normal. Your body may feel different, for example you may feel bloated or your breasts may be tender or sore. You may also feel tired, hungry or sick.

If you have some bleeding, this may not indicate a period. Sometimes when the egg attaches itself to the womb there is some 'implantation bleeding'. And if you don't have a period, this may be because it is late, or because you are stressed. It doesn't necessarily mean you are pregnant.

Taking the test

You can take a pregnancy test from the first day of a missed period, or from 21 days after you have had unprotected sex. You can take the test in a sexual health clinic or at your GP surgery. If you want to do the test privately, you can buy a kit at the chemist. You pee on a spatula (stick) when you go to the toilet, and this will detect whether the HCG hormone (which indicates that you are pregnant) is present in your urine.

The test is extremely accurate, so if it is positive, you are definitely pregnant. If it is negative but your period still doesn't start, then you should do another test a week later to make sure.

If you or your partner are pregnant it is important to talk to someone as soon as possible about your options (see Unit 7.2).

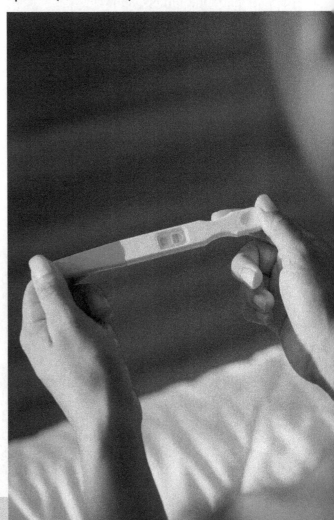

DISCUSS

Discuss the different reactions these young people have to hearing that they or their partner are pregnant.

> What am I going to do now?

> I can't believe it.

> This is terrible.

> I'm so happy.

> What will my Mum say?

> I'm in total shock.

1. Why are they so varied? What factors are more likely to make the reaction (a) positive (b) negative?

2. Do you think pregnancy is just a girl's responsibility? What about boys? Does it make a difference that boys are often emotionally and financially involved?

   Give reasons for your views.

Miscarriage

About one in five pregnancies end naturally in the first 23 weeks. This is called a miscarriage. Most miscarriages happen in the first 12 weeks, sometimes so early that you may not be aware that you were pregnant. There can be a range of reasons why a miscarriage happens, such as problems with chromosomes, or excessive smoking, drinking or drug use, but we still don't know the cause of many miscarriages. If a miscarriage happens after 24 weeks of pregnancy it is called a stillbirth.

Common signs of miscarriage are bleeding from the vagina, abdominal cramping or back pain. If you have any of these symptoms when you are pregnant you should see your GP or midwife. If you are bleeding heavily and/or in a lot of pain, you may need to go straight to A&E. The doctor will refer you to an Early Pregnancy Unit at your local hospital for a scan to see what is going on and will advise you on what to do next.

You can have all sorts of feelings after a miscarriage – upset, sadness, relief, confusion. It can be hard to talk about, but there are organisations that can help, such as the Miscarriage Association (helpline 01924 200 799).

Fertility

Fertility is the ability to conceive, which in girls begins with the first period, usually at around 12–13 years old. A woman's odds of getting pregnant are highest in her 20s, as this is when women are technically the most fertile and have the best quality eggs. As a woman approaches 40, her odds of getting pregnant decrease rapidly. The quality of the eggs decreases as well, which means a higher risk of miscarriage.

Men are not restricted to a fertile window each month, as their sperm are being formed all the time from puberty onwards. However, the quality of men's sperm declines slowly after the age of 35.

Many factors other than age can affect fertility, including medical conditions (such as polycystic ovary syndrome, endometriosis, fibroids, testicular cancer), environment and even diet.

Your lifestyle choices can affect your fertility too. Both men and women should:

- stop smoking, as smoking lowers the quality of reproductive cells
- limit their alcohol intake
- prevent, get tested for and treat sexually transmitted infections – infections such as chlamydia and gonorrhoea can cause pelvic inflammatory disease and lead to infertility.

Women should also maintain a healthy weight, as being overweight or significantly underweight can hinder normal ovulation. And talk to a doctor if you have very heavy, painful or irregular periods as they might be a symptom of an underlying medical condition that can cause infertility.

RESEARCH

Using the internet, research the options available to same-sex couples wanting to start a family, such as insemination, co-parenting, surrogacy, sperm and egg donation, fostering, adoption and IVF. Write two to three paragraphs on what you find out.

DISCUSS

What do you think a couple in their 20s should do in order to improve their chances of starting a family? Give reasons for your views.

7.2 What to do if you are pregnant

Pregnancy can be planned but it can come as a surprise. If so, it is likely to be an emotional time, when you need to think carefully about what you are going to do next.

The choices you make about a pregnancy will affect the rest of your life. If you or your partner are pregnant, there are three options:

- keep the baby
- terminate (end) the pregnancy
- go through with the pregnancy and have the baby adopted.

Each is a huge step to take, especially if you are a teenager, so you need to be aware of the facts and the implications of your decision.

Abortion – the facts

Abortion – or 'termination' – means ending a pregnancy. There may be many different reasons for choosing to do this. One in three women in Britain will have an abortion in their lifetime. The pregnancy is ended in a hospital or licensed clinic, either by taking medications or having a minor surgical procedure. Abortions are safest if they are carried out as early as possible in the pregnancy.

Beware of 'crisis pregnancy centres', which may advertise themselves as helpful, but are actually pro-life organisations that only present one set of views. They aim to persuade women not to terminate their pregnancy, rather than supporting them to make the best decision for them.

Polly's story

Polly, 17, was shocked when she found out she was pregnant.

'We always used a condom, but I suppose it split or something. I started getting stomach pains and my GP told me I was pregnant. I just burst into tears. My boyfriend couldn't believe it and didn't want to know. My mum was amazing, though. We discussed all the options and talked to a sexual health counsellor. Part of me desperately wanted to have the baby, but we agreed that I was too young to take on the responsibility.

'So, ten days after seeing my GP again, I went to hospital to have a chemical abortion. I was given a pill and had to come back two days later and take a different pill. I had cramps and a bit of bleeding but was home the same day. I was in a bit of a daze all through the experience, and very tearful for a few weeks. It was the right thing to do, but even now, months later, I get upset when I think about it.'

Fact check

There are many organisations that can give you information and support if you discover you are pregnant:

- Brook (www.brook.org.uk)
- a local sexual health clinic
- the British Pregnancy Advisory Service (BPAS) (03457 30 40 30)
- National Unplanned Pregnancy Advisory Service (NUPAS) (0333 004 6666).

The law on abortion

According to the 1967 Abortion Act, abortion is allowed any time in the first 24 weeks of pregnancy. After the 24th week, abortion is allowed for certain medical reasons:

- if continuing the pregnancy and having a baby would be worse for the physical or mental health of the pregnant person
- if the child is likely to be seriously **disabled**, physically or mentally.

Legally, two doctors have to agree that there is a serious threat to the pregnant person's health or life, or that the foetus is seriously disabled.

Since abortion is safer overall than giving birth, many doctors agree to a woman's request for abortion without needing to hear her reasons. Some doctors, however, demand specific evidence that a woman's health will be put at risk by the pregnancy.

RESEARCH

Research two of the organisations listed in the 'Fact check' box opposite.

1. What sort of support do they offer to teenagers who discover they are pregnant?

2. Which one would you recommend to a friend who was pregnant, and why?

Adoption

If you do not want to keep the child after it is born, then you can apply to have the baby adopted. An approved adoption agency would select the right family for your child. The new family would become the baby's legal parents. Your rights of contact with the child would be limited.

The decision is yours, not your parents', even if you are under 18. If the father is not named on the birth certificate, his formal permission isn't necessary. You can change your mind about giving your baby away right up to the time of the court hearing, after the baby is born.

DISCUSS

1. What might be the advantages and disadvantages of giving a baby up for adoption?

2. What kinds of feelings do you think a young teenager would have going through this process?

Keeping the baby

Keeping the baby is a lifelong commitment, so you need to think about what it really means for you and whether being a parent is something you are ready for.

Here are some questions from teenagers about keeping their baby.

‘Who can offer me help and support? It will be tough on my own.’

‘Do I need to stop drinking or smoking? What else do I need to do to look after my baby's health?’

‘How are we going to afford it?’

‘Is the child's other parent going to stand by me? What part do I want them to play in bringing up the baby?’

‘How much say am I going to have as the father?’

YOUR CHOICE

Explore the questions the teenagers above have about keeping their baby. Which do you think would be the most important factors to consider?

WRITE

Imagine that a teen got pregnant aged 15. Write some guidance exploring what they and the other parent could choose to do, and why. You could structure the paragraphs like this:

1. how they might feel

2. what support they would get

3. what option they may choose, and why

4. how they might feel afterwards.

7.3 Teenage parents

What is the reality of being a teenage parent?

So much to do as a teenage parent

It's a huge challenge to be a teen parent, but your input is vital – for your child, your partner and yourself. There are so many things you can do ...

... for your child

Your aim is to help your child have the best start in life. It may seem at first that your role is just to look after the child, but your direct relationship and bond with your baby will have a positive effect on their wellbeing throughout their life. If you are affectionate and supportive, playing with and cuddling your child, talking and reading to them, you will boost their emotional and social development. You also need to consider the relationship you have with the child's other parent.

'I had to give up most of my football and I resented that at first. But as I got closer to my son, Max, I just wanted to spend time with him and his mum.' Martin

'I didn't want the father involved at all at first. But then I did some research and realised that children benefit from having two parents to relate to. So I decided he would be involved and have some contact with his son.' Jodie

... for your partner

If you are the father or second parent, help your partner to manage the birth and the exhausting weeks afterwards. (Note, though, that it is the mother's decision who attends the birth.) The mother will be focused on the baby's needs, so you need to be supportive. Your strength, kindness and support will enhance your relationship with your partner, even if there appears to be little time and energy just for the two of you.

'I felt ignored by Susie, my partner, and there were a lot of rows. But I could see that wasn't helping anyone, including baby George, so I had to get used to a different role in her life.' Ollie

'I didn't want Mason, the dad, involved at all. But then I realised it wasn't his fault – we both had responsibility for what had happened. Gradually, I let him in – it was his child as well.' Flo

... for yourself

Friends, neighbours and even professionals can easily ask about the baby but forget about you as parents. So always ask your health visitor or social worker for help and support. Becoming a parent can be very stressful. And there is a lot to learn about parenting, so don't be too proud to access support.

'My local young parents group was really helpful in the first few months. I was the only dad there, so it was tough at first.' Kyle

'It took a while for me to get the hang of breastfeeding – I was so tired, and sometimes it was really painful. But the health visitor kept helping and encouraging me. We got there in the end!' Jenny

Fathers' rights

Fathers do not always have official parental responsibility for their children, even if they have lived with the mother for a long time. One way to ensure you do have parental responsibility is by jointly registering the baby's birth. With parental responsibility, the father has a right to make decisions about their child's care and upbringing.

If the father is not in a relationship with the baby's mother or other parent, he can still do a lot to support his child. Most fathers choose to stay connected to their children. Being respectful and supportive of the mother or other parent helps to support the baby as well. If the father's living situation is stable and safe, the more and better contact he is likely to have with his child.

Hannah's story

I got pregnant at 17. I was in complete shock and wanted an abortion, but changed my mind after I talked it through at the clinic. My relationship with my partner wasn't good, but we tried to make a go of it together.

After Brooklyn was born, my life changed completely. I got depressed and split up from my partner. My mum was a life-saver. She had raised me on her own, and knew what it was like. She got me to see my GP and I started to go to support groups.

Brooklyn is three now. I can't believe I've got him but he's totally wonderful. Juggling college and being a parent on my own is exhausting so I can't honestly recommend it. Yet I wouldn't want it any different. How amazing is that?

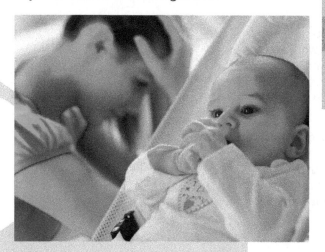

Fact check

However much teenage parents want to do the best for their child, the statistics show that life can be a struggle. For women under 20:

- they are 22 per cent more likely to be living in poverty themselves by age 30
- there is a higher risk of missing out on further education
- there are higher rates of poor mental health for up to three years after birth
- their children have a 75 per cent higher rate of infant mortality
- their children have a 63 per cent higher risk of living in poverty.

DISCUSS

Discuss what you have learned about being a young parent.

1. List all the things that change if you have a baby as a teenager.
2. What things can make life difficult for a teenage father?
3. What does Hannah mean when she says, 'I can't honestly recommend it. Yet I wouldn't want it any different'?

WRITE

Imagine that you are a teenage parent. Write three blog posts describing your experience:

1. during the pregnancy
2. the week after the birth
3. a year later.

RESEARCH

Research what support is available for young parents. Make a list of the top three sources of support that you find.

7.4 Good parenting

Being a parent or carer can be the toughest but also the most rewarding thing you ever do. It is such an important role, with many responsibilities and demands on your character and skills.

What do children need?

Baby

'I was so unprepared for the impact. Our baby Bonnie just took all my energy and attention. My partner and I were exhausted and a bit in shock for the first week or so, but have gradually got used to it. Now I wouldn't want anything different. I've got used to the way she cries when she needs attention, and I've learned to give her that attention, which calms her. We're really in love now, after a rocky start.' **Mia**

'Paternity leave wasn't really long enough, but at least I could support my partner through the sleepless nights. I bonded with baby Laurie straight away and love holding him. Changing his nappy is a chance to make contact and show that I love him. I hate being away from him now I'm back at work.' **Alfie**

Toddler

'Harper is suddenly all over the house, racing around and pulling things out of cupboards. You learn not to mind the mess, but there's a lot of clearing up to do. Just getting down and being physical with her is best. She's playing all the time; it's demanding and fascinating at the same time.' Izzie

'Harry is Mr Tantrum. I used to get really cross, but that wound him up even more. So I'm trying to stay calm and let him express his feelings – it's challenging! It's like he's testing us all the time. But we can also have a lot of fun together, and watching him develop into a little boy, talking and all, is amazing.' **Jacob**

'As a same-sex couple, we adopted, so we got Kira aged 2. My goodness this was a shock to the system! We went from no children to the terrible twos overnight. Kira really likes to challenge us. If you let her get away with something, she'll remember and try it again. So it's important to have clear, consistent boundaries with her.' **Patrick**

Primary school age

'Now Charlie's at school I've been able to increase my hours at work. The difficulty now is juggling work and home and dashing everywhere. Also, he's found it hard making friends and is even more clingy when he gets home. I try to be as patient as I can and give him space to play and talk about his day.' **Grace**

'I'm not living with Fay's mum so I'm trying to get involved in helping her at school as much as I can. I've built up a good relationship with the class teacher. Fay's into football and that's great for me, taking her to the club and working on her skills. Arguing with her about having a mobile phone is less fun!' **Omar**

Adolescence

'Zac is very mature sometimes – he comes out with amazing ideas and understanding. The next moment he can be like a toddler. My partner deals with the big mood swings better than I do: he keeps telling me about the hormones racing around Zac's body and the pressure he's under at school and so on. I understand that Zac wants to be different, but there always seems to be some conflict.' **Pippa**

'Having two mums is all our son Joe's ever known, so he's used to it. Occasionally we have to deal with a comment from a kid at school, but apart from that it's just like dealing with any normal teenager – he sleeps longer, and he sometimes needs more time than adults to think things through to express his feelings.' **Jayne.**

'I remember what it was like when I was a teenager, so I try to do a mixture of listening and allowing on the one hand, but also being clear about the ground rules on the other. You've got to pick your battles and argue for the things that really matter, not trivial stuff like messy bedrooms.' **Shaun**

DISCUSS

1. In groups, read the experiences of the parents (above) and choose one of the stages of a child's development. Make lists of:

   a) the key needs of the child at this age

   b) the key skills parents or carers need to have.

   Be prepared to make a presentation of your discussion.

2. In pairs, think about what it was like growing up at primary school, and then at secondary school.

   a) How did your parents or carers treat you differently at different stages? Make a list, and then compare your lists in groups.

   b) What stage are you at with your parents or carers now?

DISCUSS

1. What is good parenting? Read what the young people below say about their roles and responsibilities as parents. What do you think is the most important role that a parent has?

'Giving your children a good start in life, because once they are at school you become less of an influence on them.'

'Preparing your children for independence, so you are no longer needed.'

'Making sure your children are safe and healthy.'

'Ensuring that your kids get everything they need.'

'Teaching them to know the difference between right and wrong.'

'It's love and affection, isn't it? All the time.'

2. Read what Ros says, below. Do you agree with her? What counts as too much parenting, and why may that be unhelpful for children? What counts as too little parenting?

'Too much parenting is as bad as too little parenting.' Ros

What is a mother?

She's the one we turn to
when we feel lost and sad,
she's our steadying anchor,
the best friend we've ever had.

She's the one who went without
to keep us clothed and fed,
the one who dried our tears,
and tucked us up in bed.

She's the one who understood
our childhood hopes and fears,
the one who praised our efforts
through all our growing years.

Mary M. Donoghue, from *Smells of Childhood*

DISCUSS

Read the poem 'What is a mother?'

1. Does the author give a realistic picture of what a mother is? What does the poem leave out?

2. Replace 'mother' with 'father' or 'parent' and 'she' with 'he' or 'they' and read the poem again. Would you want to change anything? If so, what?

WRITE

What age of child would you look forward to parenting most and why? Write a paragraph or a poem.

8.1 Different types of partnership

The structure of families is constantly changing. Instead of getting married, many people are living together. And marriages themselves take different forms, along with civil partnerships.

Marriage

Marriage is a formal agreement between two individuals that unites their lives legally, economically and emotionally. Traditionally couples got married in a religious ceremony, but these are becoming less and less popular. Most couples now opt for civil marriages, which are performed by a government official and take place in a register office or an 'approved premises'. Note that a religious ceremony is not legally binding in itself, as you have to register the marriage and get a marriage licence to make it legal.

Supporters of marriage like the fact that it is an institution that goes back hundreds of years and is backed by religion and custom. Opponents of marriage dislike precisely the same features, claiming that it is sexist and stuck in the past. For example, until 2019 marriage certificates required the name and profession of the couple's fathers or stepfathers but not the mothers or stepmothers.

Civil partnerships

Before 2004, same-sex couples did not have the option to get married. In 2004, same-sex couples were granted the right to have 'civil partnerships'. In a civil partnership, a couple is entitled to virtually the same rights and responsibilities as they have in marriage. For example, they have the same inheritance rights, which allows one partner to pass on their property to the other when they die without paying a huge tax bill.

Since 2014, same-sex couples have been able to choose to marry or to enter a civil partnership. This legislation was extended in 2019 so that opposite-sex couples could also form a civil partnership. Couples can also choose to convert an earlier civil partnership into a marriage if they wish.

Living together (cohabiting)

Many people decide to live together instead of getting married. This is called cohabiting. Some couples cohabit for a period of time and then get married. Others cohabit as an alternative to marriage or a civil partnership, as a long-term, committed relationship.

Cohabiting couples don't have the same protection under the law as married couples. For example, moving in together does not give you automatic rights to each other's property, no matter how long you live together. And if your partner dies, cohabiting does not entitle you to inherit anything. A partner who has given up work to look after children, for example may not be entitled to anything if their partner dies. And it is possible to live with someone for decades and simply walk away from the relationship without taking any responsibility for your former partner, who may have given up work to bring up your children.

However, you can take action to avoid these problems. It is best to get legal advice if you have concerns, but it is possible to put in place legally enforceable arrangements regarding children and jointly owned property. It is also always sensible to make a will.

Fact check

There has been a gradual long-term decline in marriage rates over the last 50 years. A report from the Office of National Statistics shows that marriage rates for mixed-sex couples in 2015 were the lowest on record, with 21.7 marriages per thousand unmarried men and 19.8 marriages per thousand unmarried women. The sharpest fall for mixed-sex couples comes for men and women aged under 20.

As fewer young people get married, the average age for marriage has gone up. In 2015 the average age for a man to marry was 37.5 years, while for women it was 35.1 years.

Arranged marriages

Arranged marriages are very traditional practices in Muslim, Hindu and Sikh cultures. In an arranged marriage, the bride and groom may be suggested, chosen or approved by the two families with the consent of both parties.

YOUR CHOICE

1. Discuss why you agree or disagree with the opinion below.

'Living together is a good way to have some of the benefits of marriage without the formal and legal commitments of marriage.'

2. Read Anil's and Krishna's views on arranged marriages below. What are some of the pros and cons?

'Arranged marriages take the stress out of finding a partner, and strengthen the bonds between the two families. Love between husband and wife slowly grows, which makes for a more stable relationship.' Krishna

'Arranged marriages reduce your choice. If you really dislike the person your family has chosen, you can feel like you are being sentenced to a life of misery.' Anil

DISCUSS

'Civil partnership is a way of making a public commitment to your partner, and of showing it's an important step in your life.'

'After my parents' divorce, I am definitely not getting married.'

'You can live happily together without being married nowadays.'

'Marriage is a legal contract. It's there to protect you from being exploited.'

'Getting married takes away the freedom to do what you want to do as an individual.'

'I want children and so it's important that I am married first, to give them security.'

1. Discuss the different views about marriage, civil partnerships and other long-term relationships given above. What are your own views?

2. Why do you think young people are choosing not to marry or to marry later?

WRITE

Write a short paragraph on each of the following:
   a) marriage or civil partnership
   b) living together.

List some features of each type of partnership, then say what you think are the pros and cons of each one.

8.2 What makes relationships work?

Falling in love is one thing; making a successful long-term relationship with a partner is another. Why do we do it, and what skills do we need to do it well?

Committed relationships are good for your health

The relationships we form with other people are vital to our mental and emotional wellbeing – and therefore also to our survival. As humans, we have a natural desire to make close connections with others. A long-term, committed relationship is a golden opportunity for two people to love, support and help each other for the benefit of both. Close friendships and family relationships can also help to keep us healthier and happier.

People in healthy relationships tend to listen to each other, trust and respect each other, consistently make time for each other and engage in healthy activities together. The social and emotional support that comes with a partner is a great stress-buster – indeed, studies have shown that married or paired people produce less cortisol, the stress hormone.

Research also suggests that married people who have undergone heart surgery are three times more likely to survive the first three months after surgery than single patients. So good partnerships can help people heal. In addition, being in a loving relationship gives people a sense of wellbeing and purpose, which also has a positive effect on health.

YOUR CHOICE

Read the different benefits to being in a committed relationship identified by couples on the next page. Rank them in order from most important to least important in your own view. Then share your views with a partner and discuss why they may be different from theirs.

DISCUSS

Discuss what you learn about the benefits of long-term relationships in 'Committed relationships are good for your health'.

1. Are there any aspects of committed relationships that could be unhealthy?
2. If so, what could partners do about these?

What's the best thing about a committed relationship?

'**Companionship**. Sharing ordinary things with someone you love and building up that sharing over the years.'

'**Security**. I feel supported in the things I do. I can rely on my partner to back me up, and to be there for me. That makes me feel stronger as a person.'

'**Teamwork**. We work together and pool our resources. So financially it makes sense, but we also bring different skills to the complex task of making life work.'

'**Children**. To me, bringing up children in a relationship that is strong and reliable is the most important thing. They need that stable structure in which to grow.'

'**Love**. If you truly love someone then you'll want to spend your life with them. It's a deeper feeling than the love you can have with friends or casual partners.'

'**Developing as a human being**. A committed relationship makes demands on the couple, but precisely because of that it allows you to grow emotionally and not get stuck in a rut.'

Oiling the wheels of a relationship – the four Cs

Your relationship with your partner will not always be straightforward, but if you follow the four Cs, it will run much more smoothly.

- **Communication**. Communication means talking. It's vital to communicate your thoughts and feelings with your partner, not just about important or difficult issues but on a day-to-day basis. Telling them about the little things going on in your life will build up a bond of companionship and trust. Communication also means listening and respecting your partner's point of view.

- **Consideration**. Respect and consideration are the bedrocks of a solid, loving relationship. Being considerate means trying to take your partner's wishes into account, and thinking how you can make life easier for them. Even when you have differences – and there will be differences – you need to respect those differences.

- **Compromise**. Compromise means being willing to find the middle ground between two viewpoints, which may seem poles apart. A successful relationship is not about getting what you want all the time. If you want to win all the time that will mean that the other person loses all the time, which is bad news for the relationship. It's the sensible and adult solution to meet half way on those occasions when you disagree.

- **Cooperation**. Cooperation means working together. That doesn't just mean doing your share of the household chores. It means supporting each other through thick and thin, and trying to make things work out for the good of the partnership and the family. A partnership is a team, and the most successful teams are those that cooperate the best.

YOUR CHOICE

Which of the four Cs do you think is the most important in keeping a relationship together? Write a paragraph giving your reasons.

DISCUSS

Look at the following scenarios. Discuss what you would do in each situation. Give reasons for your views.

1. Your partner is fed up with you going out with your friends for a third night in a row, and wants you to stay in to have a meal together.

2. Your partner is the only one loading and unloading the dishwasher and emptying the rubbish. You work full time and they work part time, so you feel this is fair.

9.1 Social media and body image

With social media, there is more pressure than ever for young people to conform to a certain image. At every moment of the day, you can see other people's posts, and photos and know that they will be looking at yours and forming opinions about you.

Social media

Social media can be a lot of fun. It's good to catch up with friends and share photographs and news about our lives. However, we don't always get a true picture of people's lives from what they post on social media. Most of us choose to share the photos where we look the best, and may even use a filter to make ourselves look that little bit better.

With most social media sites, people can like and comment on what you have posted. While it is nice to get feedback from people, a desire for likes and comments can become addictive.

It is easy to start judging ourselves by what we see on other people's social media. For example, you may worry that you don't have as many friends or followers as other people do, but if someone has 500 followers it is unlikely that they are all genuine friends.

DISCUSS

Look at the following statements about social media. Which ones do you agree with? Why?

'Social media likes aren't real life – we should concentrate more on what is happening around us in the real world, not on the internet.' Maryam, Mansfield

'Social media is a great way of finding out what is going on in your local area, your country and the world – all at the sametime.' Lucinda, London

'You can't say somebody is a real friend on social media until you have actually met them in real life.' Amy, Nottingham

'Most of the photos on social media aren't real – they've been digitallyenhanced.' Tomas, Norwich

Body image

You may feel that you are expected to look a certain way, dress a certain way and act a certain way, according to your age, gender, background and where you live.

YOUR CHOICE

1. How do you think your views of what is the ideal body image are formed?
2. What pressures are there on you to conform to such an image? Where do they come from?
3. Is there the same amount of pressure to conform, whatever your gender?

The unrealistic model

Digitally enhancing photographs using techniques like airbrushing and Photoshopping contributes to the unrealistic expectations people have of how they should look. Airbrushing is when a photo or image is altered to remove any flaws, such as blemishes or stretch marks.

In some cases, such as the two photos below, the way a model looks at the start of a photoshoot, with less makeup and with no digital enhancement, can be completely different from the way they look in the end photo.

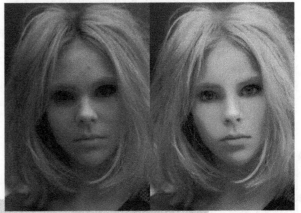

1. Read through the list of digital techniques that can improve the way a model looks in a photo. Which do you think are acceptable? Which are not? Give reasons for your views.

   a) Changing the lighting on a model's face or body.

   b) Changing the skin tone of a model to make them more or less tanned.

   c) Adding 'makeup' to a model digitally to make them look more attractive (for example, smoothing skin or adding colour to the lips).

   d) Changing a model's hair to give them a different look.

   e) Changing how fat or thin a model looks by digitally altering their waistline.

   f) Making a model look more muscular than they really are.

   g) Changing the colour of a model's eyes.

   h) Changing the size of a model's eyes, nose or lips.

   i) Making a model's legs longer or thinner.

   j) Smoothing out a model's skin tone and removing blemishes and wrinkles.

2. What other possible digital changes can you think of that would be acceptable or unacceptable?

In 2011 a project from Global Democracy and Idea 9 suggested that there should be a global international standard disclaimer to say when a photograph has been digitally enhanced. Using the internet, research this disclaimer. Do you think this is a good idea? Give reasons for your views.

Does it matter who we see in the media?

Some commentators have argued that it matters who we see in the media, as they provide important role models. Therefore, if society is made up of people of different ethnicities, who are fat and thin, young and old, able bodied or disabled, then the models we see should be the same, so we get a realistic view of what people's bodies are actually like.

Real Beauty – getting it right and wrong

In 2004 and 2005, the soap brand Dove ran its first Real Beauty campaign. This involved using real women of all shapes and sizes to advertise its soaps. The idea was to get away from the stereotype of all female models being tall and thin, to show a variety of women of realistic shapes and sizes. The advert was well received.

However, the same brand Dove was criticised in 2017 for publishing an advert on Facebook where a Black woman takes off a brown T-shirt, as if to reveal she has a white T-shirt underneath, but in fact it is a different, white, woman who is revealed wearing the white T-shirt. The advert was accused of being racist, and Dove apologised, saying it had 'missed the mark' when designing the advert.

1. Do you think it is important that we have people who look realistic and who look like us in adverts?

2. Do you think adverts should reflect the cross-section of the society that views them?

3. Do you think you would feel differently about yourself if you saw more models as they really look?

4. Can you find any examples of digitally altered images of men? Do you think men are judged as much as women on their looks, clothes and bodies?
   Give reasons for your views.

10.1 Eating disorders

An eating disorder is a serious mental health condition that will often require professional treatment.

There are different types of eating disorder, including anorexia, bulimia and binge eating disorder. Each eating disorder has its own symptoms, but all will usually involve eating too much or too little and becoming obsessed with weight and body shape.

What causes someone to develop an eating disorder is a complex subject, and will vary from person to person. Scientists are still exploring the role of genetics and biological factors in this process.

Anorexia and bulimia are both eating disorders and mental health conditions.

Anorexia

Anorexia, or anorexia nervosa, is an eating disorder where people severely limit or avoid food and may try to lose as much weight as possible, in order to become thinner. A person who has anorexia tries to keep their weight as low as possible by not eating enough food. They may have a distorted body image and feel that they are fat even when they are very thin. They may also over exercise, sometimes to an extreme degree. However, because they are not eating enough they will lose muscle as well as fat.

Doctors diagnose someone as anorexic once they have lost 15 per cent of their normal body weight. As anorexia is a mental health condition, doctors will treat both the physical and psychological symptoms of the disorder.

There are almost 700 000 people in the UK suffering from anorexia. It occurs most in teenage girls, especially between 15 and 19. While 90 per cent of diagnosed anorexia sufferers are girls, 10 per cent are boys. This means there are 70 000 men and boys with anorexia in the UK, and the numbers are growing.

Emma Woolf, in her book, *An Apple a Day*, writes about anorexia from a personal perspective:

'It's when we're all together [my family] that I feel most trapped by my illness. I want to join in, I want to share the fun and eat with them but it's been so long. I've forgotten how. Gripping my mug of black coffee more tightly, I feel distinctly not part of the family. (If they offer me a slice of cake I feel awkward, and if they don't bother to offer me any I feel angry.) I want to be part of all that rowdy, pleasurable eating but I can't.'

Bulimia

Bulimia, or bulimia nervosa, is a combination of binge eating and then taking measures not to put on weight. Bulimia can be a difficult problem to spot. People suffering with bulimia still eat food, but they are afraid that they are going to put on weight. They may binge eat, but then use different methods to lose the calories.

Bulimia can be dangerous. It has been linked to tooth decay, gum disease, throat infections and mouth ulcers. In addition to this, a person doesn't absorb all the vital minerals and vitamins from their food that are necessary to stay in good health.

Treating anorexia, bulimia or an eating disorder

Both anorexia and bulimia can become an addictive habit, and they both need to be treated as mental health problems. Forcing someone with anorexia or bulimia to eat food or follow a diet plan is not a sustainable long-term solution on its own. As with other eating disorders, the key to treating these conditions is to help the person to think and feel differently about themselves and their circumstances. They can then try to develop a more healthy relationship with food and eating. However, it is unlikely that someone will be able to manage to do this on their own and they will need to have professional support.

Signs and symptoms that you may have an eating disorder

It is not always easy to spot the signs of an eating disorder in ourselves or in others. Symptoms will vary from person to person. However, if you or someone else is regularly doing any of the following this may be a sign of an eating disorder:

- spending a lot of time worrying about looks, weight and body shape
- avoiding social situations where people will be eating and drinking
- eating too little
- eating too much
- developing an excessive and rigid exercise regime, and feeling like a failure if you don't stick to it
- thinking constantly about food, dieting, and the number of calories every type of food contains, and having strict habits or routines around food
- feeling guilty about eating too much or too little food.

If you are concerned about yourself or anyone else showing these symptoms, it is important to seek help. As a first step, talk to a trusted adult, visit your GP or call the BEAT (Beating Eating Disorders) helpline on 0808 801 0711. Seeking professional help as soon as possible is essential.

11.1 Youth crime

Every year thousands of children aged 10 to 17 commit crimes ranging from fare-dodging, graffiti posting and petty theft to burglary, criminal damage and knife crime. Most of the crimes are committed by boys.

Reasons for committing crimes

There are many different reasons why young people get involved in crime.

- There is a lot of pressure on young people to dress and behave in certain ways. These pressures can lead them into crime.

- Many young people have very little money. They see crime as a way of getting the money to buy things that they couldn't otherwise afford.

- Some young people are lured into crime by criminals who give them presents then blackmail them into getting involved with illegal activities such as delivering drugs.

- Others have difficult situations at home. This can make them so angry and frustrated that they express their dissatisfaction with their lives by turning to crime.

- Gangs can provide a sense of belonging for a young person missing this at home, becoming part of person's identity and seeming to offer them protection.

- For some young people, it is a way of challenging authority. They decide to push the boundaries as far as they can, including by committing crimes.

- Some young people get involved in crime because they have nothing better to do or enjoy the adrenaline rush they get from doing something illegal. It brings adventure and risk into their lives.

'If we want to empower children to be resilient to the lure of gangs and make different choices, we need to ensure they have a relationship that enables positive decisions.' Anne Longfield, Children's Commissioner, 2019

DISCUSS

Which do you think are the main reasons why young people get involved in crime?

Can you suggest any other reasons?

ROLE-PLAY

What causes one person to give in to the temptation to commit a crime while another person does not?

Role play a scene in which two people are planning to do something illegal and putting pressure on a third person to join them. Take it in turns to be the person who is reluctant.

Youth courts

If you are aged 10 to 17 and are charged with committing an offence, you will be tried in a youth court.

If you are 16 or under, a parent or guardian must attend the court with you. It is also worth considering getting a solicitor to speak for you in court.

You will be tried by a panel of three magistrates and a legal clerk. After hearing all the evidence, they will find you guilty or not guilty. If you are found guilty they will decide what sentence to give you.

Natalia's story

Natalia was 13 when she was caught shoplifting in a department store.

I'd never have done it on my own, but Katie said it was easy. She'd done it a couple of times. She knew the top I wanted for the party and she wanted some shorts. We'd bought a couple of small things, so all we needed to do was to slip the clothes into the store's bags and walk out.

We'd only gone a few paces when a security guard stepped in front of us. She marched us back into the shop. It felt like everyone was watching us. It was so embarrassing.

The security guard told us she knew we had been shoplifting. There was CCTV footage of us taking off the price tags and stuffing the things in our bags.

She said she'd call our parents to come and collect us. By now I was crying. I felt so ashamed. What if she called the police?

Then my mum and Katie's mum arrived. I could see how upset Mum was. I was sobbing. I felt like I'd let the whole family down.

The security guard explained what we'd done. To my relief said she'd decided not to involve the police this time as the items weren't very expensive. We had to pay for the clothes as we'd removed the tags. We were banned from going into that department store for a year.

I wish I'd stopped to think of the consequences before going along with Katie's suggestion.

DISCUSS

1. How does Natalia feel? Do you think she will have learned from her experience and won't shoplift again?

2. What is your attitude to shoplifting? Is stealing from a shop different from stealing from someone's home?

3 'Shoplifters should always be reported to the police.' Do you agree? Give your reasons.

What sentences can youth courts give?

Youth courts deal with serious cases such as theft and burglary, antisocial behaviour and cases involving drugs. The sentence given will depend on a young person's age, the seriousness of the offence, whether they have a criminal record and whether they pleaded guilty or not guilty.

The court will also take into account any mitigating circumstances, such as problems you may be experiencing at home.

The sentences include:

- a discharge
- a custodial sentence
- a reparation order, which can involve apologising either in person or in writing to the victim of the crime and repaying them what you took from them
- a criminal behaviour order (CBO) to stop antisocial behaviour; this can last up to three years.

RESEARCH

1. Find out exactly what happens in a youth court. What do the different sentences above mean?

2. Think of the questions you would want to ask if you were summoned to attend a youth court. Write out the questions and the answers.

YOUR CHOICE

Study the cases below. What sentence would you give from the following options?

a) a discharge

b) a custodial sentence

c) a reparation order

d) a CBO

Case 1 Trevor was arrested for drunken and threatening behaviour towards people in the town centre.

Case 2 Kester was selling MDMA tablets at a festival.

Case 3 Ameena was caught stealing an old lady's purse.

Case 4 Khaled broke into a neighbour's flat and tormented their cat.

Case 5 Toni sprayed graffiti on a bus shelter.

11.2 Gangs and knife crimes

Belonging to a gang can give you status, but it causes problems. You may be drawn into criminal acts and be threatened by people with knives or other weapons.

Gangs

You may feel that by joining or working for a gang you'll be protected, but this isn't true. Belonging to a gang often means that you are in danger of being targeted by other gangs.

There's the danger, too, that you will be involved with something illegal and find yourself in trouble with the police.

You may also be at risk if you try to leave the gang. (see Unit 6.2)

Why do people join gangs?

There are often several reasons why people join a gang.

- It gives them a sense of belonging which may be missing in their life.

- It builds their confidence. They may feel more powerful now that they have a group who will stick up for them.

- They feel they will gain status by belonging to a gang. They join so that they'll get respect.

- There is pressure on them from either a family member or their friends.

- They are tricked into joining by criminals who groom, trap and exploit them.

- They feel they have no alternative, living where they do.

A 2019 report by the Children's Commissioner found that young people involved with gangs were more likely to

- have social, emotional and mental health issues

- have a parent or carer misusing drugs or alcohol

- not have their basic care needs being met at home

- have witnessed domestic violence

- be missing or absent from school.

Here are two young people's views.

'It's better to be on the inside than the outside. You know not to mess with certain people because they're in a gang. But when you're with your boys and the others are walking past you, they won't even look in your direction.' Jess

'Once you're in, that's it. It's no good thinking that if you don't like what they're doing, you'll just leave. It doesn't work like that. They'll come after you.' Ray

YOUR CHOICE

What do you think are the main reasons some teenagers join gangs? Rank the reasons in order, starting with the most common reason. Then share your list in a class discussion. Are other people's lists different from yours?

Ask Erica

Dear Erica

I was being bullied, so I joined a gang to protect myself. But the things other members of the gang do worry me. They sell drugs and there are always fights going on with other gangs. Now I want to get out. But I'm scared what they'll do to me, or to my family.

Emeralda

Dear Erica

I'm being pressurised by my friends to join a gang. They say that everyone on the estate should be a member. What should I do?

Declan

WRITE

Write Erica's replies to Emeralda and Declan.

Knife crime

Carrying a knife is a criminal offence, whether or not the knife is used to harm someone. You can be searched by a police officer if they think that you are carrying a knife. It makes no difference if you say you were only carrying it for self-defence.

Fact check

The following sentences apply for carrying or using a knife.

- For the first offence, if the knife is used in a threatening or offensive manner, a minimum six months in jail for an adult, or four months in jail for a young offender under 18.

- For a second offence carrying a knife, a minimum six months in jail for an adult, or four months in jail for a young offender under 18.

- The maximum sentence for an adult carrying a knife is a four-year jail sentence and an unlimited fine.

- Longer sentences can be imposed if a person is carrying a more dangerous weapon, such as a machete.

In groups, discuss these suggestions for how to reduce knife crime. Which do you think would be most effective? Which do you think would be least effective?

a) Have tougher penalties for offenders.

b) Introduce curfews for under 18s.

c) Encourage people to hand in knives and other weapons by having an amnesty.

d) Employ security firms to patrol streets and give them powers to stop and search.

e) Find ways to help young people feel safe on the streets without a weapon.

f) Ban the sale of knives on the internet.

g) Encourage parents and carers to discuss with their children the consequences of carrying a knife and the benefits of taking responsibility and choosing not to.

Teenagers talking about knife crime

'Carrying a knife means I know that I can defend myself if necessary.'

'People won't bully you or disrespect you if they think you've got a knife.'

'It's a tiny minority of teenagers who carry knives.'

'If people know you've got a knife, they are more likely to attack you. Carrying a knife doesn't make you safer, it puts you in more danger.'

'It's your duty to report anyone you know who carries a knife.'

Study the statements above about carrying knives. Discuss each one and say why you agree or disagree with it.

What is joint enterprise?

Joint enterprise means that you are there when a serious crime, such as a murder, is committed or you do something that leads to or helps that crime to be committed. This means you could also be charged with that crime. For example, your presence or your actions as a member of a gang involved in a fight where a gang member uses a knife can lead to you being charged with a very serious crime.

How can you avoid being charged under joint enterprise?

- Don't carry a knife or other weapon.

- Don't get involved in disputes between gangs that could lead to violence.

- Consider the consequences of your actions. Don't wait until it's too late and you are in serious trouble.

Role play a parent or carer talking to their son, who is angry because he has been threatened with a knife and wants to start carrying one himself.

12.1 Fake news

Fake news means news stories that are untrue in some way and aim to mislead people.

Newspapers and news websites may exaggerate a story because they want to sell more copies to their readers, get more 'hits' on their site or increase the number of times a story is shared on social media.

They may also present a story from only one viewpoint, leaving out some of the facts. This is known as bias.

Some fake news stories are completely untrue. In these cases, the story has usually been created deliberately, for a purpose: for example, to persuade people to vote for a particular politician or political party.

Fake news can be used deliberately to strengthen or damage a person, company or country, or to promote a viewpoint. For example, lies might be told about the number of immigrants committing crimes or claiming benefits.

DISCUSS

1. Why do you think Trump's press secretary lied?

2. What do you think can be done in such situations, where both sides accuse each other of broadcasting fake news? Give reasons for your views.

Case study: The size of the crowd

In 2016, President Trump became the 45th President of the United States of America. In January 2017, he was sworn in at a ceremony known as his inauguration. When questioned about the ceremony, Trump's press secretary, Sean Spicer, told reporters that the crowd that had come to see the ceremony was the largest for an inauguration of a US president.

In fact, this was fake news. Photos showed that the crowd was only about one third of the size of the crowd that had attended President Obama's inauguration eight years before. Trump's supporters and his opponents both accused each other of disseminating (spreading) fake news, even though one side was lying and the other telling the truth.

President Trump's inauguration

President Obama's inauguration

Fake news on social media

Fake news has become a problem in recent years due to the increased use of social media. This is partly because everyone can now be a 'reporter'. Anyone can write something or share a photo on Twitter, Instagram, WhatsApp or Facebook and present it as news. False news stories can be shared very quickly on social media platforms.

In some cases, this is done on an industrial scale, with countries or companies disseminating fake news to advance their agenda. This is sometimes done by paying hundreds of people to post fake news on social media as their full-time job. For example, during the 2016 US election, it was discovered that dozens of United States political news websites had been launched from the small Macedonian town of Veles. Almost all these sites supported Donald Trump, mostly with fake news stories which were then shared via Facebook.

Responsibility for fake news

Over the last few years, there have been calls for companies such as Facebook and Instagram to take responsibility for the information they allow to be posted and shared by users on their platform. Facebook's response has been to say they now have more staff responsible for taking down fake news where it is clearly identified. However, like extremist material (see Unit 12.2), fake news can clearly still be found all over the internet.

Case study: Anti-vaccination

The anti-vaccination, or anti-vaxxer, movement is an example of a movement that is doing serious harm by spreading false information around the internet. Anti-vaxxers are people who believe that vaccinations are a human rights violation. The movement is based on the work of disgraced scientist Andrew Wakefield, who inaccurately claimed in a scientific paper in 1998 that the MMR (measles, mumps and rubella) vaccine could cause autism in young children. This has been disproved by further scientific studies – there is no scientific link between vaccinations and autism. However, this hasn't stopped the anti-vaccination movement from claiming that there are all sorts of problems with vaccinations.

Vaccinations have wiped out an entire disease, smallpox, and save millions of lives each year by preventing people from suffering from diseases like measles, rubella, whooping cough, typhoid and polio.

However, now too many people are not vaccinating their children because they believe the false information put out by the anti-vaccination movement. The Royal Society for Public Health estimated in 2019 that half of parents with small children had been shown anti-vaccination information on social media. As a result, there have been outbreaks of preventable diseases such as measles in the UK, which can be very serious, causing brain damage and even death.

DISCUSS

In groups, consider the following questions. Which do you think are the most useful to help you decide whether information online is true or is fake news? Why?

1. Check the source – who are the creators of the site or the news article and where does the information actually come from?

2. Does the text agree with itself throughout, or are their contradictions?

3. Do other sources or stories from other independent news organisations on the internet support the news story you are reading?

4. Is the story just factual, or does it contain opinions? If it contains opinions, whose are they and why have they been included?

5. Does the website or source look professional, or does it look amateur and hastily put together?

6. Does the website or source have a good reputation for producing honest, independent reporting?

7. If the post includes a photograph, are there other photographs of the same event which tell the same story, or do some tell a different story?

8. If the post includes a photograph, are there any obvious signs that it has been edited or tampered with?

12.2 Radicalisation

Radicalisation is the process through which a person is persuaded to support extreme views.

A person is known as a radical when they want to make extreme or fundamental changes to society. Some radicals can be dangerous.

Radicals may support one of a wide variety of groups that believe in violent revolution, such as neo-Nazi groups on the extreme right of British politics, or extreme Communist groups on the far left of British politics. Other radicals may support Islamist terrorist groups such as Daesh (so-called Islamic State), or violent pressure groups such as the Animal Liberation Front, who believe in using violence to stop animal testing.

Prevent radicalisation

The Prevent strategy was launched by the Labour Government in 2006 to tackle radicalisation across society, as part of its counterterrorism programme. It has several aims:

- to challenge the ideology of terrorism and those who support it

- to protect vulnerable people from becoming radicalised

- to support sectors and institutions where there are risks of radicalisation.

A major part of Prevent is to stop young people being drawn into supporting terrorism.

Andrew's story

I got into trouble after the London Bridge attacks. I saw a photo on the internet of a Muslim woman walking past a dying man just ignoring him. It made me angry. I began to look at other websites criticising Muslims. The more I saw, the angrier I felt. I got talking to this girl in a chatroom about it. She said bad things about Muslims and I found myself agreeing.

I talked to more of her friends, and started feeling very anti-Muslim. Things came to a head when I insulted a Muslim boy at school, calling him a pig.

The school referred me to their anti-radicalisation programme. I had several meetings with a counsellor and was advised to do some research about the photo I had seen originally. I found out it was posted by a fake Twitter account traced to Russia – the Russians were trying to increase anti-Muslim feelings in the UK. The woman was walking past because she was traumatised. We also found out that the girl I'd been chatting to online had been a fake identity for a neo-Nazi called Mike.

I was shocked and embarrassed. It took quite a while to fully accept what had happened to me. I've learned a lot from the experience though. Now I'm careful to check where online stories and photos have come from.

DISCUSS

Read Andrew's story and discuss the questions below.

- What mistakes did he make?

- What did he do right?

- What would you do in such a situation?

- What more could be done to tackle radicalisation in this case?

Kamran's story

Kamran is 14 [...] Social workers picked up on comments he made in support of Osama Bin Laden, joining Daesh and killing Americans. His school were aware of wider communication and behavioural difficulties, including autism. His mother was also very ill, and he had unsupervised access to the internet.

The local authority referred Kamran to the Channel programme and with the consent of his parents he was taken on as a case and given a mentor, Daud, who was a youth worker.

Daud, as well as encouraging Kamran's passion for football, talked with him about Islamic teachings and accompanied him to the mosque. He helped Kamran see the positive aspects of being the only Muslim pupil at the school, and explored the possibility of holding an Islamic awareness day. Daud worked with Kamran's parents to build family relationships and manage internet usage, while the Channel programme organised for local Prevent officers to raise awareness of extremism and radicalisation at Kamran's school.

Over a period of time, there was a steady improvement in Kamran's behaviour at school and at home. Kamran no longer made extremist statements and learned to speak to his father if he saw something that he did not understand.

Reproduced from the *Educate Against Hate* website

DISCUSS

Read Kamran's story and discuss the questions below.

1. What different factors made Kamran vulnerable to radicalisation?

2. What has helped him take a different view?

What you can do

There are some things you can do to protect yourself and others against radicalisation.

1. If you think someone is trying to spread hateful views and/or encourage people to harm others, this might be radicalisation. Talk to somebody you trust, such as an adult where you live, the police, a teacher or a member of the safeguarding team at school. If you don't want a face-to-face conversation, contact the police online or get in touch with a helpline like the NSPCC.

2. Keep talking to family and friends. Radical extremists like to isolate their targets so that they only get their news and information from them, and they can shape their target's views.

3. If you suspect someone close to you is trying to radicalise you, try to surround yourself with people not involved in the situation. If necessary, use the internet away from home to seek help.

4. Be aware of grooming. This is where someone will give you favours and attention to gain your trust. Once you begin to trust them, they may start to persuade you to agree with their views.

5. Avoid chatting to anonymous people on the internet and giving out your personal details to people you don't know.

6. Avoid stereotyping others. Not all White people, Black people, Christians or Muslims behave or think in the same way – we are all individuals. Stereotyping is often used as an excuse to take action against a group of people.

7. If you come across or are shown material on the internet glorifying violence or terrorism, tell someone you trust such as a parent, carer or teacher.

DISCUSS

Which do you think are the best ways of protecting yourself from radicalisation? What other ways can you think of? Give reasons for your views.

WRITE

In pairs, compose an email for your headteacher to send to all Year 10 students. It should include five bullet points about radicalisation, what the signs might be and how to prevent it. You might find it useful to visit the Educate Against Hate website.

Fact check

Terrorism-related offences carry the following maximum prison sentences:

- preparing or helping to prepare an act of terrorism – life imprisonment
- collecting information helpful in preparing an act of terrorism – 10 years
- distributing material that encourages an act of terrorism – 7 years
- not telling the police you know someone is preparing an act of terrorism – 5 years.

12.3 Online literacy and responsibility

Online literacy means having the ability to spot fake news (as discussed in Unit 12.1) and understanding that you need to be careful about what you share and say on the internet.

A person is legally responsible for anything they write online and any pictures that they post. This means that you have to take responsibility for what you write or post. If you are unsure about whether you should write, post or share something, err on the side of caution, and keep the material to yourself.

Remember what you post now, even within a private group, could one day be seen by a potential employer, college, university or partner.

DISCUSS

Look at the following types of behaviour. Which do you think are acceptable? Which should you not be doing? For which should you ask someone else's permission first? Give reasons for your views.

1. Sharing an article online without first checking whether it is true.

2. Forwarding to someone else a private email that was sent to you, without the permission of the person who wrote it.

3. Posting a photo on Instagram of a friend or family member who looks silly, with a funny caption, without their permission.

4. Revealing another person's personal, political or religious views on the internet, with or without their permission.

5. Tagging a photo of someone looking drunk at a party.

Social media and the law

Social media posts from years earlier have led to people in public life losing their jobs. They are also being referred to in more and more legal cases. The police are using social media to catch criminals, since social media posts are now regarded as a valid form of evidence.

Some examples

- In 2019, actor Oluwaseyi Omooba was sacked from her role in the UK stage show of *The Color Purple* for homophobic comments she had made on Facebook five years earlier.

- In 2017, Labour MP Jared O'Mara was forced to resign from his role on the Women and Equalities Select Committee because of sexist and homophobic comments he had made on online forums thirteen years earlier.

- In 2014, a man from Bristol was sent to prison for sending a series of abusive tweets to two female MPs.

- After the riots of 2011, two men were sent to jail for sending tweets encouraging others to damage property and celebrating acts of vandalism.

- In 2017, the columnist Katie Hopkins was ordered to pay a six-figure sum of money in damages to the food blogger, Jack Monroe, after she successfully sued her for libel (saying something untrue about her) in a tweet she posted.

- In 2018, a drug dealer was imprisoned after a fingerprint identified from a photo taken in a private WhatsApp group connected him to a legal case.

- A WhatsApp message was also used as part of the evidence to convict a man of a firearms offence, as a WhatsApp message to his girlfriend suggested he had a gun.

The fact that social media can be used in court against a person shows how important it is to be careful what you write on social media, especially in the heat of the moment.

Case study 1 – Social media and terrorism

In March 2019, a white supremacist from Australia shot and killed 49 people and injured more than 40 in a terrorist attack on two mosques in Christchurch, New Zealand. As he was committing this atrocity, he live-streamed himself on Facebook so people could see what was happening in real time. His video was then copied and shared many times on YouTube, Twitter, Facebook and other social media platforms. Some traditional media companies shared clips of this stream on their websites and in their news coverage. They were strongly criticised for this action, and some quickly took down the footage as a result.

Forty-eight hours later, a man was caught in the UK sharing the footage and glorifying this act of terrorism on social media. He was immediately arrested and charged with distributing malicious material via the internet.

Case study 2 – Self-harm material

In 2017, the social media platform Instagram, which is owned by Facebook, came under sustained criticism for not removing material that promoted self-harm and in particular, suicide, on its pages. This was drawn to the attention of the government. As a result, the Health Secretary, Matt Hancock, argued that social media firms ought to be doing more to remove such material from their sites. The government proposed new laws and rules to govern the behaviour of social media companies. Instagram apologised, and stated that its rules do not allow such material to remain on its platform. However, it is still possible to view such material online.

WRITE

In pairs, draw up a list of things that people should and should not do online that can be used as a code of conduct for using the internet in your school. Give reasons for each of the points in your list.

Social media and responsibility

In early 2019, public pressure grew on social media companies to do more to control the content hosted and shared on their platforms. MPs investigated the issue, and were alarmed at the range of material they found featuring or promoting self-harm, pornography and hate speech. As a result, there have been continuing calls for social media companies to do more to remove harmful content from their sites, and new laws to regulate their behaviour have been proposed.

Under planned new laws, an independent regulator will have powers to impose fines on companies, to ban sites from search engines and even to block their access to UK users.

Codes of practice will be drawn up requiring firms to act to prevent and take down illegal content, such as terror or child abuse images, within fixed timescales and to remove material promoting self-harm and suicide.

Prime Minister Theresa May said, 'For too long companies have not done enough to protect users, especially children and young people, from harmful content. Online companies must start taking responsibility for their platforms.'

YOUR CHOICE

Who do you think is responsible for protecting children from disturbing content and dangerous or false information online?

- Is it their parents/carers?

- Is it the government?

- Should social media firms themselves be responsible?

- What about the people who publish the information (who post it on the social media websites) – should they be held legally responsible?

Give reasons for your views.

13.1 Attending to your wellbeing

The term wellbeing refers to a whole group of positive feelings about yourself and the world.

These feelings include happiness, contentment, enjoyment, self-confidence and connection with the world. Good mental wellbeing also gives you the resilience to cope when times are harder than usual. So it is an important ingredient of good mental health.

Wellbeing is not something we have – like pocket money or nice clothes. It may be more helpful to think of it as something we do – 'being well'. So the more we do to build it up, the stronger a resource it is in our lives.

Children less happy with their lives, report finds

If you try to gauge the happiness of children by the smiley faces they post on social media pages, a major survey of children's wellbeing should make you think again. It identifies a significant decrease in their happiness with life as a whole and with friends between 2010 and 2016.

The Good Childhood Report 2018 brings together the findings of a major study carried out by the Children's Society in partnership with the University of Leeds. The survey asked thousands of children questions about their lives and what made them happy and unhappy.

The report shows that girls are unhappier with their lives than boys. Also, children attracted to the same or both genders have significantly lower wellbeing than other children, with almost half of them self-harming.

Key factors for wellbeing seemed to be the connections that children had with those around them, such as family and friends. They needed to feel supported and at ease with their identity in these groups. If they were bullied or felt they had to conform with expectations that were at odds with their own identity, then their wellbeing suffered.

DISCUSS

Read the newspaper article. Why do you think the wellbeing of children has declined in recent years?

Consider these factors: social media, appearance, pressure to fit in with society's expectations, friendships, school, gender stereotyping, family relationships.

YOUR CHOICE

Answer the quiz questions opposite to see how good you are at maintaining your mental wellbeing. Keep a record of your answers. Then check your score and discuss with a friend what you have learned about yourself, and what you could do to help yourself.

What are you doing to improve your wellbeing?

1 Having fun. Doing things that cheer you up is an obvious way of feeling better. How often do you let yourself feel happy, for example by being with friends who make you laugh, or treating yourself with something you like?

a) often, **b)** sometimes, **c)** hardly ever/never

2 Self-esteem. Accepting yourself as a person builds your resilience. How good are you at feeling OK about yourself even when you don't achieve your aims, or when you get criticised?

a) pretty good, **b)** sometimes good, sometimes not, **c)** not very good

3 Eating well. Your diet is more important for mental health than you may think. Do you:

a) have a balanced diet, **b)** have slightly too much unhealthy food/drink, **c)** have a lot of junk food and sugary drinks?

4 Sleep. Not enough sleep, or poor-quality sleep, affects our energy and mood. How is your sleep?

a) good (9+ hours per night), **b)** average (7–8 hours), **c)** poor (6 or fewer hours)

5 Getting active. Physical exercise is a mood-booster. Regular walking is just as good as aerobic exercise. How often each week do you exercise for 30 minutes?

a) most days, **b)** some days, **c)** rarely/never

6 Sharing your feelings. Talking to someone you trust about how you are makes problems more manageable and builds emotional intelligence. How good are you at sharing your feelings?

a) I often do this, **b)** I sometimes talk about how I feel, **c)** I always keep my feelings to myself

7 Connecting with others. We are social beings, so developing good relationships with family, friends and community is vital to our wellbeing. How much effort do you put into your relationships?

a) a lot of time and effort, **b)** a fair amount of time and effort, **c)** not much effort at all

8 Hobbies and interests. Learning new skills keeps us mentally alert and interested, and connects us with others. What time do you give to learning new skills or to your existing hobbies?

a) a lot, **b)** some, **c)** hardly any/none

9 Giving to others. Kindness and helping others gives us a sense of purpose and strengthens our relationships. Volunteering, helping someone or even just a kind word – every little helps. How much do you give to others?

a) a lot, **b)** some, **c)** hardly anything/nothing

10 Being aware of yourself and the world. Practising mindfulness (see Unit 13.2) can help us enjoy the world and manage stress. For example, how much do you really notice what's going on in the present moment – in yourself and in the world around you?

a) I regularly take time to notice things,
b) sometimes I stop and notice how I am feeling,
c) I always race from one activity to another

What's your score?

Mostly **a**s: You are doing lots of valuable things to help your mental wellbeing.

Mostly **b**s: You are doing some things to help your mental wellbeing, but there is more you could do if you wanted to.

Mostly **c**s: There are plenty of things you could do to improve your wellbeing. Visit the Mind and Young Minds websites to find out more.

YOUR CHOICE

1. Discuss what Sarah Stewart-Brown says about wellbeing. Do you agree?

'No one can give wellbeing to you. It's you who has to take action.' Sarah Stewart-Brown, professor of public health at the University of Warwick

2. What can *you* do to build or maintain your wellbeing?

- List or draw five key things you are already doing that contribute to your wellbeing.
- Then list or draw five things you could do to improve it.

13.2 Mindfulness

Mindfulness means allowing ourselves to see the present moment clearly.

If we notice what is going on in our bodies and our minds, as well as in the world around us, it can change the way we see ourselves and improve our mental health and wellbeing. There are many ways in which we can practise mindfulness.

Why practise mindfulness?

It brings a more helpful and flexible attitude towards painful thoughts and feelings. 'When I get anxious, instead of panicking about my racing heart, I sort of just notice what's going on. That tiny space allows me to calm down.' Zoe

It allows us to be more present. 'Mindfulness helps me get out of my head. I'm much more aware of the world around me.' Joel

It helps us relax. 'Focusing on my breathing a few times a day has really helped me de-stress.' Beau

It encourages kindness. 'I'm much more patient with myself and others now. I don't beat myself up any more for feeling sad.' Darcey

It allows us to change our thought patterns. 'I'm looking at my thoughts and feelings differently. I don't get so caught up in thoughts like "I'm rubbish". It's just another thought, after all.' Ellie

It's a powerful self-management strategy. 'I don't lose it so often now when people say hurtful things about my appearance. I can take a breath and react in a more effective way.' Mikey

It allows us to be more focused. 'I'm not as distracted as I used to be, so I can stick at things for longer.' Noah

YOUR CHOICE

1. Read the young people's experience of practising mindfulness. Which area or areas of your own wellbeing do you think could be improved if you followed a mindfulness practice?

2. Try out the mindfulness exercises on these pages.

   Research others, such as mindful breathing, mindful eating and the body scan, on the internet or via a mindfulness app.

   Then choose one of these to commit to over a period of at least a week. Write down how you feel at the beginning of the week and at the end, as a way of evaluating your experience.

Watching the thought train

When there's a lot going on in our lives, we can get very caught up in our thoughts. These are often about the past, going over previous events. Or they may be about the future, such as planning what we're going to do next. Either way, we aren't really present in the here and now, and we are likely to be distracted or stressed. So, beginning to 'just notice' our thoughts can be a helpful way of bringing us back to the here and now, and feeling more settled or grounded.

'Watching the thought train' is a way of distancing yourself from all the thoughts that may be carrying you away. Follow these steps:

1. Feel the real contact of your feet on the ground.

2. Begin to notice your breathing, where it feels the strongest, for example in your belly or nostrils. Bring your attention to your breath in this way as you settle yourself down. When your thoughts leap away, gently bring them back to focusing on your breath.

3. After a minute or two, switch your focus of attention to the thoughts themselves. Imagine you are standing on a station platform watching a train go past. Each thought you have is a carriage of the train. Notice it coming to your mind and notice it leaving.

4. The train may go fast or slowly, it doesn't matter. It may even stop – but probably not for long. Try to hold on to the sense of yourself on the platform just watching the thoughts go past.

DISCUSS

1. Practise 'Watching the thought train' by being silent for three minutes, preferably with your eyes closed.

2. Next, read what Sofia and Alex experienced (below).

3. Then discuss what your own experience was when you watched your thought train.

4. 'You can't stop the waves but you can learn to surf.' Jon Kabat-Zinn. Discuss what Jon Kabat-Zinn means, and why learning 'to surf' is important.

'It was hard at first to not get on each carriage and be carried away by the thoughts. After a few practices I noticed I was getting back on the platform sooner and sooner. It was weird seeing all those thoughts race past me.' Sofia

'I tried to put my thoughts on the train and send them away, but more and more kept coming. It was stressful. Eventually I remembered that mindfulness isn't about making the thoughts go away, and I relaxed a bit. Then I was calmer and even enjoyed stepping back from it all.' Alex

WRITE

1. Take a ten-minute mindful walk. It could be your walk home from school, or the walk to the bus stop. Walk a bit more slowly than usual and really engage your senses of sight, hearing, smell and touch. Try to notice ten things that you wouldn't normally notice. When you get back, write down (a) what you noticed, (b) how you felt.

2. Pay attention to your feelings through the day. On your phone or a piece of paper, record how you are feeling in the morning, at midday, in the afternoon and the evening. Write down where you notice the emotion in your body, for example in your chest or in your stomach, and how you express it (if you do). Keep this going for a week.

RESEARCH

Research some mindfulness apps. Try them out, then draw up a personal pros and cons chart for two different apps.

13.3 Mental illness

Everyone has mental health. It affects how we think, feel and behave. It also helps us make decisions and relate to others. Mental ill-health, or mental illness, is one aspect of mental health.

A spectrum of mental health

It is helpful to imagine a spectrum of mental health, with healthy at one end and unwell at the other. Just like with our physical health, we move up and down this spectrum. Lots of factors can affect how we move along the spectrum, such as our home or school environment, difficult life events, and physical factors such as the quality of our sleep and diet.

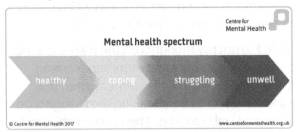

Reproduced by permission of the Centre for Mental Health.

We all have bad days – perhaps we feel like crying for no reason, or we can't cope with the simplest of tasks. But sometimes our low mood seems to last for a long time and it's hard to shift it. If so, you may have a mental health problem and need some help to feel better (see Unit 13.4).

Different names for different problems

Mental health problems are usually defined carefully so that professionals can give people the appropriate care and treatment. These are some of the common mental health problems that can affect children, teenagers and adults:

- **Depression** is when your mood is very low, so that it is hard to enjoy life. People with bipolar disorder, a type of depression, swing between high and low moods (see Unit 13.6).

- **Anxiety** can take many forms, such as anxiety in social situations or extreme concern about your physical appearance (see Unit 13.5).

- **Obsessive compulsive disorder (OCD)** is an anxiety disorder in which someone has obsessive thoughts and compulsive behaviours (see Unit 13.5).

- **Attention deficit hyperactivity disorder (ADHD)** is a behavioural disorder where someone has difficulty paying attention and can be hyperactive and impulsive.

- **Eating disorders** include disorders such as anorexia, bulimia, over-eating and binge eating (see Unit 10).

- **Self-harm** is when someone harms themselves. It is usually a way of coping with or expressing intense emotional pain (see Unit 13.6).

Some people experience 'psychotic' symptoms, which may include hallucinations, such as seeing, hearing, smelling or feeling things that no one else can.

Myths about mental illness

MYTH 1: *Mental health problems happen to other people.*

FACT: According to the World Health Organization, one in four people will experience a mental health problem every year. Official statistics suggest that mental health problems affect about 1 in 10 children and young people, and are more common in adolescence. NHS research published in 2018 shows that nearly 400 000 under-18s in England are being treated every year for some sort of mental health condition.

MYTH 2: *People with mental health issues should just get over it.*

FACT: Mental health problems are real, accompanied by real changes in the chemicals in the brain. They are not trivial or a sign of weakness, even if there isn't an obvious physical symptom to show for it. They need to be treated seriously, not dismissed.

MYTH 3: *It's an embarrassment to have a mental health problem.*

FACT: Many people feel embarrassed about mental illness. They think they will be treated differently and lose friends. But why should it be more embarrassing than having any other illness? It is not a failing on the part of the sufferer.

MYTH 4: *People with a mental illness are dangerous.*

FACT: Some high-profile violent crimes involving people with a mental illness give the wrong impression. The vast majority of people with a mental health issue do not harm others.

DISCUSS

1. What have you learned about mental health from what you have read here?

2. 'As a society we must no longer adopt a "stiff upper lip" attitude ... we need to talk openly about mental health, something that affects us all directly.' Paul Farmer, former Chief Executive of the charity Mind

   Why does Paul Farmer say this? Do you agree with him? If so, what can we do as individuals to change society's attitude to mental health?

RESEARCH

Research what Prince Harry and Prince William have said about their own mental health problems. What effect do you think their speaking out has had on helping other people with mental illness?

DISCUSS

Opposite is a questionnaire in a self-help book aimed at teenagers. Read it and then answer these questions.

1. Why are you asked to think about your mood over a period of two weeks?

2. Are there any questions that surprise you, or that you think are missed out?

What's your mood?

Think about your mood over the past two weeks. How much do you agree with the following statements about your mood? Give a rating between 1 and 10 for each one, where 1 = completely disagree and 10 = completely agree.

1 Over the last two weeks you've had little interest in doing the stuff you usually enjoy doing.

2 Over the last two weeks you'd describe your mood as down, low or hopeless.

3 Over the last two weeks you've had trouble falling asleep or have trouble getting out of bed (even on a non-school day!).

4 Over the last two weeks you've lacked energy and feel tired all the time.

5 Over the last two weeks you've had little appetite or found yourself comfort-eating.

6 Over the last two weeks you've felt like a bit of a failure at work, home or school.

7 Over the last two weeks you've found it hard to concentrate on work or even things like watching TV.

8 Over the last two weeks you've noticed a change in your mannerisms – you feel either slow and sluggish or buzzing and hyper.

9 Over the last two weeks you've thought about harming yourself or thought about your own death.

10 Over the last two weeks your mood has made it difficult for you to do your normal day-to-day activities.

Add up your score. If your score is higher than 50, can you say why? Are you having a bad time of it at the moment? (For example, if you're having a break-up you may well score over 50.) If you CAN'T identify a life event or a reason why you might be feeling so blue, perhaps it's time to think about your mental wellbeing.

Do the questionnaire in another two weeks – has anything changed? It could be that a couple of days off, or being kind to yourself, is all you need right now, but MAYBE it's time to seek some support. There's plenty of it out there (see Unit 13.4).

Adapted from Juno Dawson, *Mind Your Head*

13.4 Getting help and giving help

We all need help and support at some point in our lives. Sometimes we are in a position to help and support others.

Getting help

If your mood has made it difficult for you to do your normal day-to-day activities, then you need to seek help.

Talk to someone

Talking to someone is an essential first step on your road to recovery. Talking may even be all you need to do to turn the corner. Try to talk to someone you like and trust, such as one of the following:

- a friend
- a sibling
- a parent or carer
- another relative, such as an aunt or grandparent
- a friend's parent
- a teacher or school nurse.

Professional organisations

Talking will give you a different perspective, a shoulder to lean on, and perhaps some advice about what to do next. But you cannot expect your friends or family to be experts in mental health issues. You could speak to the school counsellor or contact any of these organisations for more advice or support if necessary:

- Childline: call free on 0800 1111, speak to a counsellor online or visit the 'explore' section on their website.
- The Mix: offers free and confidential support to the under-25s. Their free helpline (0808 808 4994) is available 4 p.m. to 11 p.m. Monday to Saturday. Email and webchat support are available on their website.

- Samaritans: offers free and confidential help in the UK 24/7. Call free on 116 123 or email jo@samaritans.org.

Be careful how you use the internet. Trustworthy advice and forums can be found on the websites above, as well as at the Young Minds, Kooth or NHS Mental Health websites.

More formal support

When advice isn't enough, or when the advice suggests that you need to go down a more formal route, it is usually best to start by contacting your GP. You may want to go with a trusted adult or someone else for moral support and to listen to the advice with you, but you don't need your parents' or carers' consent. The meeting will be confidential unless the GP feels that you or someone else may be harmed.

The GP will ask you lots of questions and suggest what to do next. This could be making some simple self-help changes in your lifestyle and keeping an eye on the situation before coming back for another chat. Or you could be offered medication to help with depression and anxiety, or tablets to help with your sleep. Medication will be a short-term solution to take the edge off the difficulty while you find better ways of coping and other sources of support.

You may also be referred to the Child and Adolescent Mental Health Services (CAMHS). These are local, specialist mental health support teams run by the NHS. The services are free and help young people under 18 who have emotional, behavioural or mental health problems.

In an emergency

If you feel that you, or someone you know, needs urgent help and may be at risk of harming themselves or others, you should contact your GP, or visit your local NHS walk-in centre or closest A&E department straight away. If necessary, phone the emergency services on 999.

RESEARCH

Explore the two websites Kooth and The Mix. If you were suffering with a mental health problem, which site would you turn to first, and why?

DISCUSS

'When I had an eating problem I spent hours each night on chatrooms and forums. Talking to other people who felt the same as me seemed like a life-saver at the time. It was only later, when I saw my GP and started treatment, that I looked back and wondered how helpful it was. There's something unhealthy about being locked in a "room" with people who all think and feel the same.' Faisal

'Finally discovering people who felt the same as me was such a relief. I wasn't "weird" after all! It also felt good being able to help others by sharing my story. I wasn't just a victim of my panic attacks, I was something bigger than that. It was an online buddy who suggested I try CBT [cognitive behavioural therapy], which was the best thing I did.' Maya

1. Discuss Faisal's and Maya's experiences of using social media to help them with their mental health issues.
2. List three advantages and three disadvantages of using forums and social media in this way.

Giving help

Supporting a friend – Dos and Don'ts

Colin Letts gives you some tips on how you can help a friend struggling with their mental health

Do listen. Really be present for your friend. They will feel supported and valued by you if you simply acknowledge what they are feeling and thinking.

Don't judge. It's not your friend's fault that they may have mental health issues. Being criticised or dismissed will not help their mood and will mean they lose you as a source of support.

Do spend time doing fun and healthy things with them. Go shopping or to the cinema, play sport or exercise together – there are lots of non-talking activities that may boost your friend's mental health.

Don't try to solve their problems. There may be some advice you can give, such as 'you need to talk to the school counsellor', but your role is mainly to give emotional support and to listen.

Do keep in touch. Even if you are shocked by what your friend is saying, keep supporting them. They need your support, and one day you may need theirs! Check in with them regularly to see how they are.

Don't take it on all by yourself. You can only help your friend if you are strong enough yourself. If you feel out of your depth, or that they are at risk of serious harm, you need to ask for help from a trusted adult. In some cases, a professional's opinion is **essential**.

DISCUSS

What are the three best tips in 'Supporting a friend'? Compare your ideas with those of others.

ROLE PLAY

In pairs, role play a conversation between friends where one of you has been feeling very low for the last fortnight. Then swap roles. Finally, feed back how the conversation felt for both of you.

13.5 Managing anxiety

Anxiety is an emotion closely related to fear. You could say that fear is what we feel when there is a danger *right now* and anxiety is what we feel when we are concerned about something happening *in the future*.

The fear/anxiety emotion is extremely important, as for tens of thousands of years it has helped us to respond to any situation that we think may be dangerous.

Anxiety is an automatic reaction, controlled by the central nervous system. When we are anxious, our bodies go into 'fight, flight or freeze' mode. The idea is that if we fight, or run away, or freeze, we are more likely to survive an attack (or whatever the threat is).

There are three kinds of 'symptoms' (signs) that we may notice when this anxiety/fear reaction is set off – physical sensations, thoughts and urges (an urge is a desire to take action):

Physical sensations, for example:

raised heart beat

sweating

butterflies in the stomach

tension in neck, legs, shoulders

tight chest/shallow breathing

light-headedness.

ANXIETY

Urges, for example:

to avoid something or someone

to seek reassurance

to check/be on the alert

to hide

to get irritable or aggressive.

Thoughts, for example:

'What if ...?'

'I won't be able to cope with ...'

'It'll be terrible ...'

Anxiety conditions

Anxiety is not a disease. At a normal level, it is not a bad thing. On the contrary, the anxiety reaction is one of the most important ways we regulate our emotions to keep ourselves alive and effective in the world. *Too much* fear or anxiety, however, can prevent us acting effectively. Unfortunately, our attempts to get rid of the feeling (for example, by worrying or by avoiding situations) can make the problem worse in the long run.

For example, if you suffer from social anxiety, you will worry about social situations and being judged by others. Thoughts about 'not coping' will make you feel distressed. So, typically, you will try to avoid or escape from social situations as much as you can, or keep yourself 'safe' by various means (avoiding conversation, looking for escape routes and so on). But these actions make social anxiety worse.

Likewise, if you suffer from obsessive compulsive disorder (OCD), you will have obsessive thoughts. You will try to combat or 'neutralise' the thoughts by certain repeated behaviours (compulsions), such as repeatedly checking that you locked the door behind you. But these behaviours only make you feel better for a little while, and introduce another set of problems.

Managing anxiety

It is our attempts to *control and avoid* anxiety that can turn ordinary anxiety into an anxiety disorder. Instead, it helps to bring *mindfulness*, *acceptance and non-avoidance* into our experience by:

- being in the present and focusing on the world as a whole, not just our anxious symptoms

- seeing thoughts as just thoughts, and sensations as just feelings

- moving towards things that we want rather than running away from things we fear

- finding ways of coping with the anxious feelings until they peak and subside.

Of course, this is hard to do on your own. If you feel in the grip of an anxiety condition you may need professional help from a therapist. Getting in touch with your GP should be your first step.

Noah's story

My anxiety began when I was 11 and started secondary school. The classes were so big and I found it hard to make friends. One day I got laughed at by a group of classmates for saying the wrong thing and it was terrible. I got more and more anxious about being in groups. I kept my head down in school, and stopped going out. I kept thinking I was going to be picked on or judged. Schooldays were a nightmare of tension and sweating in fear of being noticed. But when I was alone at home I just felt rubbish about myself. I started missing school, so the school suggested that I start seeing a counsellor, and that's when things started to turn around.

The school counsellor was great. She helped me understand what was going on, something she called 'social anxiety'. I was avoiding situations because I was feeling so anxious, and that sort of kept me safe but made it all worse as well. We did a lot of mindfulness activities and I began to notice my anxious thoughts and feelings rather than just being overrun by them. We worked on what I really wanted to do, which was to go to school, make friends and join the drama group as a stage hand. We took it all step-by-step. I used the phrase 'Here's anxiety, but it's just thoughts and feelings', when I got anxious, and learned to focus on what was going on around me. I still have setbacks but I'm making a few friends and school is OK.

DISCUSS

1. In pairs, discuss what you have learned about anxiety from these pages.

2. a) What symptoms of anxiety did Noah show?

   b) How did he react to these symptoms?

   c) How exactly did he bring mindfulness, acceptance and non-avoidance into his experience of social anxiety?

3. How can you help yourself if you are suffering from high levels of anxiety?

RESEARCH

1. Research the different anxiety conditions, for example by checking out the websites of Anxiety UK and Epic Friends.

   a) Choose one anxiety condition and describe its symptoms, using a diagram of physical sensations, thoughts and urges, like the one on the previous page, to organise your ideas.

   b) What can the person do to help themselves manage this anxiety? What treatments are best if self-management is too difficult?

13.6 Managing depression

Depression is one of the most common types of mental illness. Nearly 80000 children and young people in the UK suffer from the illness. One in four people will probably suffer from depression at some point in their life.

Symptoms

The key feature of depression is low mood, which lasts over a prolonged period. Our emotional 'weather' changes all the time – we have good days and bad days, good hours and bad hours. But when we seem to be stuck in a consistent low mood, that's more than just the weather – it's the climate.

When you are in this mood, you don't want to do the things you enjoyed before. Your sleep, energy and concentration can be affected. You feel miserable and hopeless and are very often self-critical. In some cases, you may want to self-harm or have suicidal thoughts.

Causes

Depression can happen as a reaction to something, like bullying or difficulties at home. It is a natural response to big losses, such as a break-up or a death. Or it can result from the build-up of lots of little things. Sometimes hormonal changes can make us feel depressed.

Anyone can get depressed – it's a perfectly normal part of being a human for many people.

Treatment

There's a lot you can do yourself if you can catch depressive feelings before they become too fixed. Exercise is a great mood-buster, especially if it's outdoors. Make sure you share your feelings with someone you trust, or at least express your feelings in writing or art. Mindfulness practice can help you get a distance from the thoughts and feelings (see Unit 13.2).

If you are not managing to cope on your own, and especially if you are wanting to harm yourself, you must get help. Going to your GP is a good place to start. If they think you are suffering from depression, they may suggest talking regularly with a counsellor or therapist. Or they may prescribe medication, such as anti-depressants; these are pills which artificially lift your mood until you feel well enough to cope on your own.

WRITE

Draw a diagram of the symptoms of depression, listing thoughts, feelings and urges, like the one for anxiety (see Unit 13.5).

Managing negative thoughts

When you are low it is very common to blame yourself for things, or focus on aspects of yourself that you don't like. It's so important that you break this cycle! Colin Letts suggests some tips.

1. You need to be kinder to yourself in these difficult times, not harder on yourself. Do something kind and healthy for yourself and say, 'I deserve this'.

2. Be aware of the labels you are using for yourself. If you wouldn't say it to or about your best friend, then don't say it about yourself.

3. Give your negative internal voice a name. The sillier the better, like 'Bubbles'. Then, when you hear it pipe up again, have a little conversation with it:

   'I'm such a rubbish person.'

   'Oh, there you are again, Bubbles. I wondered when you'd turn up. I'm busy right now. You keep talking nonsense if you like and I'll get on with other stuff!'

4. You don't have to believe your negative thoughts. Practising mindfulness will help you to see the thoughts for what they are – just mental events.

5. Get a perspective. If your best friend heard you making that criticism, what would they say instead?

Self-harm

A tragically high proportion of young people self-harm. It needs to be talked about and faced head on.

What is self-harm? It's a physical response to emotional distress. It could be anything that harms the person in order to cope with emotional pain. Perhaps the harm makes us feel in control of a situation. Or it's a sign of desperation and a cry for help. Or it is a way of expressing angry feelings about oneself or the world.

The act of self-harm can make a person feel better – but only temporarily. The brain produces endorphins, chemicals that help us manage pain and make us feel good. Once the self-harmer has come down from the high caused by the endorphins, they can feel worse again, and full of shame or confusion. But the body 'remembers' the endorphins and so there is an urge to repeat the experience and get the good feelings again.

People who are self-harming may be feeling very distressed. So allowing the sufferer a non-judgemental space to talk is essential. If a friend of yours reveals that they are self-harming, let them talk about their feelings. Help them to think about their self-harm as a problem to be sorted out rather than a shameful secret. Tell them that professionals understand more about self-harming these days and will treat them with respect and care, if they ask for help.

Ask Erica

Dear Erica

I've been self-harming for two years now, usually when I feel really bad about myself. My parents always seem to be criticising me and I can't bear it. When I self-harm, I'm distracted from the pain of not being good enough, but that doesn't last long. I can't seem to break the cycle.

Adam

WRITE

1. Write Erica's reply to Adam.

2. What are the warning signs of depression? Design a display for a student notice board in school, including advice on what to do. Look at the Young Minds website for guidance.

YOUR CHOICE

Discuss things you can do to help yourself if you are suffering from depression. Design a self-help card and keep a copy of it on your phone. Include a list of the people you can talk to. Put the best person to talk to at the top of the list.

14.1 What is gambling?

Gambling is a popular leisure activity, covering arcades, betting, bingo, casinos, lotteries and gaming machines. Many of these activities have online equivalents.

The nature of gambling has changed in recent years. The National Lottery and online gambling have replaced football pools, bingo and horse-racing as the most popular forms of gambling.

Fact check

The Gambling Act 2005 defines gambling as 'betting, gaming or participating in a lottery'. You have to be 18 years old to gamble in adult gaming centres, betting shops, casinos and online. These premises must have a licence to provide gambling activities. Sixteen-year-olds can take part in the National Lottery and some non-commercial gambling. Some gaming machines, like coin pushers and low-stakes fruit machines, can be played by anyone.

- In 2018, 46 per cent of people in Great Britain reported that they had gambled in the last four weeks.

- In the same period, 18 per cent of people had gambled online in the last four weeks. Although gambling overall has declined in the past few years, rates of online gambling are growing.

- The gambling industry took nearly £14.5 billion from punters (people placing bets) in the year to September 2018.

- The National Lottery contributed £1.5 billion to good causes in the same period.

- The chance of winning the National Lottery jackpot is 1 in 45 million. The chance of winning any National Lottery Lotto prize is 1 in 9. (Source: *National Lottery website*)

Source: Gambling participation statistics from the Gambling Commission annual report 'Gambling participation in 2018: behaviour, awareness and attitudes'. Gambling Industry Gross Gambling Yield/Return to good causes statistics from the 'Gambling Commission Industry Statistics 2018'.

The National Lottery

Since its introduction in November 1994, the National Lottery has been hugely popular. Around 70 per cent of adults have played the National Lottery in the last year. Operated by Camelot, it raises around £30 million per week for good causes, such as sports and arts projects. For example, the National Lottery contributed almost £2.2 billion towards the funding for the London 2012 Olympic Games and Paralympic Games. Lottery tickets and scratch cards can be bought by anyone aged 16 or over.

Critics of the lottery argue that it should not be run as a profit-making venture and that the licence to run the lottery in future should go to a non-profit-making organisation. They also say that the introduction of the lottery has led to the creation of a gambling culture, in which more people are interested in and addicted to gambling. In particular, it encourages lots of the poorest members of society to spend money they cannot afford on lottery tickets rather than essentials, such as food and clothing.

Where each pound spent on a lottery ticket goes

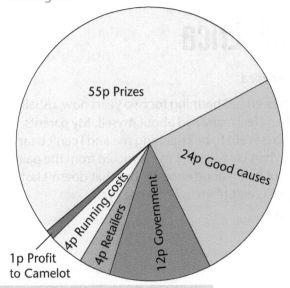

55p Prizes

24p Good causes

12p Government

4p Retailers

4p Running costs

1p Profit to Camelot

1. Do you think introducing the National Lottery was a good idea?

2. What do you think of the criticisms that are made about the way it is run and the influence it has had?

Teenage boys twice as likely as girls to gamble for money

An extensive survey on gambling among 11- to 16-year-olds has revealed some shocking statistics. Of those questioned, 14 per cent had spent their own money gambling in the past week, a figure which was higher for boys (18 per cent) compared to girls (9 per cent). This equates to 450000 young teens across Great Britain.

Ipsos Mori, the survey company, questioned nearly 3000 11- to 16-year-olds. Their report, 'Young People and Gambling 2018', shows that the average amount of their own money that young people spent on gambling was £16. The top three reasons that teens gave for getting into gambling were 'to try to win money' (46 per cent) and 'because it's fun' (44 per cent). Private bets (for example, with friends), National Lottery scratchcards and fruit or slot machines were the most common forms of gambling.

The research suggests that nearly 2 per cent of 11- to 16-year-olds are problem gamblers, and more than 2 per cent are 'at risk'. Obviously more needs to be done to educate young people about the law – and the dangers – of gambling.

Discuss the newspaper article.

1. Why does its headline emphasise that boys are more likely to gamble than girls?

2. What other features of gambling among teenagers stand out in the article?

3. What headline would *you* choose for the article?

Why do young people gamble?

'It's glamorous. You see people in films gambling and you want to be like them.'

'It's exciting. You're taking a risk and it gives you a real buzz to see if you've won.'

'I've got a friend who just can't stop – he's addicted. So he can't help gambling now.'

'It's an easy and fun thing to do when you're bored.'

'Winning lots of money is what everyone wants to do, isn't it?'

Why might people gamble?

- In pairs, collect as many ideas as you can, and rank them in order of importance.

- Compare your ranking with that of another pair.

- Then write a paragraph explaining your findings.

Read these opinions about gambling. Where do you stand? Be prepared to give reasons for your views.

'Most gambling is fun and harmless. It also raises millions for charity through the National Lottery. There are far worse things to worry about.'

'Gambling is a mug's game. It's the betting shops and casinos that are the winners. It's bad for the individual and bad for society.'

'If you're watching football live, it makes the game more exciting if you can place bets as the match is happening.'

14.2 Problem gambling

For some people gambling can lead to major problems – addiction, problems around money, friends and family, and mental health.

What is problem gambling?

About 2 million people in the UK are thought to be at risk of harm through gambling. And that doesn't include 400 000 who have developed a serious gambling disorder.

Problem gambling has been called the 'hidden addiction' because the physical effects of the problem are hard to spot. Yet someone's gambling problem can be very stressful for them and for their friends and family.

Chris's story

Chris is 14 and already addicted to arcade machines.

'I started playing the machines when I was 11. All my friends were doing it and I didn't want to be left out. When I won, it was so exciting. All the noise and lights! So I went back the next day on my own, and before I knew it I was hooked.'

Chris spent all his money and savings on his habit. He even stole money out of his mum's purse. Because he had no money left to spend on anything else after gambling, he was eventually caught shoplifting, and was forced to address the problem seriously.

Chris is not alone. Nearly 2 per cent of 11- to 16-year-olds are classified as problem gamblers, and a further 2.2 per cent as 'at risk'.

What turns gambling into problem gambling?

Gambling alters the person's mood and state of mind, making them feel excited and giving them a thrill when they win. As the person becomes used to this feeling, they keep repeating the behaviour, gambling more to try to achieve the same effect and feel the same exhilaration.

As with other addictions, the person begins to develop a 'tolerance'. This means that they need to gamble more to get the same 'high'. Sometimes this results in 'chasing' their losses, thinking that if they continue to gamble they will win back the money they have lost.

It's a particular concern for young people because teenage brains are hardwired to love risk.

Fact check

There are many different factors that may lead someone to develop a gambling addiction. You are more likely to develop a problem if:

- there is a history of problem gambling in your family
- you started gambling at an early age
- you are in a period of stress, loneliness or emotional upheaval
- there is peer-group pressure or easily available opportunities
- you have, or someone close to you has, money worries
- you are taking medication or have a condition that affects impulse control.

Research also shows that speed of play is a significant factor. Games where there is a short time between placing a bet and seeing the results present a higher risk for players, for example on slot machines.

Gambling and gaming

400000 British teens lured into under-aged gambling through video games

More than 400000 British teenagers have been lured into under-aged casino-style gambling through their video gaming, an investigation has revealed.

The children, aged 13 to 18, have been able to gamble winnings from their video gaming on websites where they can bet them for cash on roulette wheel spins or other games of chance.

The online gambling, which is illegal for under 18s, has been made possible by the creation of virtual items called 'skins', modified weapons or costumes that players can win or buy in video games.

Now Parent Zone, an advice service for parents and schools, is demanding urgent action to close the loophole that allows skins to serve as a digital currency that can be gambled and cashed out.

Giles Milton, Parent Zone's head of content, said its investigation showed gaming firms were not doing enough to stop it: 'It is gambling and children should not be gambling online. Parents need to understand what their children are doing with their money.'

There are concerns the trade in skins – of which there are 6bn in circulation worth an estimated £10bn – could itself be fuelling the rise in addictive gaming among teenagers.

From the *Daily Telegraph*, 28 June 2018

Beware of loot boxes

Teenage blogger Marcus says ...

Loot boxes (also known as crates, chests, cases and bundles) are a very worrying aspect of e-gaming at the moment. You may have come across them in games like Star Wars Battlefront 2, FIFA Ultimate Team and Overwatch. They allow players to pay – often with real money – for a chance to win virtual prizes for in-game playing.

I think using these features should count as gambling because the player is risking something of value (either real money or in-game coins) in the hope of winning something else.

Even if you are not spending real money, loot boxes encourage risk-taking and gambling-style behaviour, which could be very harmful to you later in life.

WRITE

How can fruit machines and other forms of gambling lead to addiction?

Design a flow chart, to be displayed in a youth club, describing the possible dangers that can lead to addiction. Choose either arcade gaming or online gaming as your focus.

YOUR CHOICE

Discuss the following views. Do you agree or disagree with them? Give your reasons.

You can lose loads of money on skins gambling. It's basically a gateway to real money gambling, they just cover it up because you use the skins (virtual goods) instead of currency.

Virtual items like skins and loot boxes have no financial value, so paying for them is not gambling.

14.3 How to manage gambling

There are things that we can do – as a society and as individuals – to manage gambling.

We need to look at the influence of the media, and to spot the signs of problem gambling, both in ourselves and in others, in order to be able to manage gambling.

We should be protecting our children

According to a study by the Gambling Commission, 80 per cent of children had seen gambling advertisements on TV, 70 per cent on social media and 66 per cent on other websites. Why are these numbers so high? We should be protecting children from gambling adverts.

Gambling and betting companies are not allowed to advertise to young people, but it's a fine line to draw – what counts as advertising to young people? And companies *are* allowed to advertise during sports matches, which are watched by millions of young people.

Nearly half of the top 20 football teams in Britain were sponsored by gambling companies in 2018, which means that fans see players wearing their sponsors' logos on their kit.

Fact check – the media and gambling

Gambling adverts in the UK rose from 234 000 in 2007 to 1.4 million in 2012.

The Gambling Act 2014 gives guidelines on responsible gambling advertising.

- Only licensed gambling operators can advertise.
- Advertising must not be aimed at children or leave vulnerable people open to exploitation.
- Advertising must display the Gambleaware website address.
- TV advertising should usually be after the 9 p.m. watershed (although this does not apply to sport betting during sport fixtures).

DISCUSS

In 2018 the Labour Party called for a complete overhaul of the laws around gambling ads, including a ban on gambling during live sporting events and a 1 per cent tax on the profits of gambling companies. This could be used to treat more gambling addicts.

Do you think the gambling advertising guidelines need to change? If so, why? And how?

Spot the signs of a gambling problem

Are you spending more than you want to on gambling? Or borrowing or even stealing money to fund your habit? These are just some of the signs to look out for.

Maybe you need to gamble with more and more money to get a buzz, or you find yourself chasing losses. Maybe you are losing sleep or feeling depressed over gambling.

You could be arguing with friends or family over your habit, or even missing school because of gambling.

Spotting the signs is the first step in helping you tackle the problem.

Now get to grips with the problem

Sometimes avoiding situations makes good sense – avoid friends who are gambling, avoid clicking on the links in online ads, switch off TV ads.

Then replace these things – and the buzz of gambling – with more healthy and fulfilling experiences.

Try thinking in a different way about gambling. Remind yourself of the downsides of gambling. Make a list of the good things you want in your life and put it somewhere you will see it.

You can also learn to stay in control instead of reacting on impulse.

Stay in control

All urges pass if you let them. When the urge to gamble hits you, try one of these strategies:

1. Give yourself 15 minutes before you act on the urge. In that time, distract yourself by doing something else. When the 15 minutes is up, see if you can add another 15 minutes. Repeat until the urge passes.

2. Focus on your breath and mindfully notice how the urge affects your body and your thoughts. Visualise the urge as an emotional wave that you can surf. Follow the wave as it rises and breaks, and eventually loses its power.

3. Contact organisations which you gamble through, asking them to no longer accept your money.

How to help someone with a gambling problem

Sometimes a friend will spot the problem before the gambler does, because the gambler persuades him or herself that everything is fine. What if that friend is you?

Let your friend who is gambling know that you care about them, rather than being judgemental or hostile. You need to show them that you are on their side if you want to avoid an argument. Try phrases like this:

'I'm upset because you're my friend and I don't want you to hurt yourself.'

'This doesn't seem to be making you happy at the moment. How can I help you?'

'I think what you are doing is really risky. Tell me about what's going on.'

Then listen carefully to what they say. Try to be calm and caring but also firm. Definitely do not lend them money.

Apart from talking to your friend, there are other things you could do to help:

- Let a family member or a member of school staff know what's going on.

- Suggest that the friend contacts GamCare or Childline.

WRITE

Write a list of ten top tips to help young people control their gambling that you could post on social media.

DISCUSS

Chloe catches Nadia stealing money from her purse. Nadia admits that it is to repay a loan she took out to play online poker.

1. How might Chloe be feeling in this situation?

2. What could she do to help Nadia? Think about the things she could say and the actions she could take.

RESEARCH

Visit the Gambleaware, GamCare and NHS websites. What advice do they offer about gambling problems and gambling addiction? Is the advice easy for young people to understand?

ROLE-PLAY

Two friends are planning to pool their money to go to the amusement arcade and play the machines, sharing any winnings. They are putting pressure on another friend to join them. In threes, discuss why this friend may not want to join them, and what she or he could say. Then take it in turns to be this friend and practise different ways of justifying saying 'no'.

15.1 Consumer rights

As a consumer, you may be shopping for goods (buying things) or services (buying a skill, such as a haircut). Whether you are buying goods or services, you have rights that are protected in law.

Your rights when shopping

Fact check

Under the Consumer Rights Act 2015, the law says that goods must be:

- of satisfactory quality – defined as what a reasonable person would be happy with, given its price

- as described – it must fit the description on the package or sign, or that given by the seller

- fit for purpose – it must do what it is supposed to do, and last a reasonable length of time.

The law applies to second-hand and sale goods as well.

If the goods you buy are faulty in any of the ways listed in the fact check box, you have 30 days in which to demand a full refund. After this period, the business only has to offer a repair or a replacement. If you buy digital content, there is no automatic right to a full refund – generally, you will be offered a repair or replacement, or a partial refund.

If six months passes before you return your goods, then you have to prove that they were faulty when you bought them.

You have fewer rights if you are buying from a private seller. In this case, you can only complain if the seller misleads you about the goods you are buying.

True or false?

- You can't get a refund on something you buy in a sale.

  FALSE: If the item is faulty or shoddy then your rights are the same as if you bought it at full price.

- You have to send the goods back to the manufacturer if they are faulty.

  FALSE: If you bought the goods in a shop, then the shop has to sort out the problem.

- If you are buying a service, like a haircut, you have fewer rights.

  FALSE: Under the Consumer Rights Act, the hairdresser has to provide the service with reasonable care and for a reasonable price, or the advertised price. If it's a bad haircut you can ask for it to be improved, or claim a price reduction.

- You need a receipt to claim a refund.

  FALSE: You just need proof that you bought the item. That could be a bank statement.

- After 30 days shops can't offer any refunds

  FALSE: Although it's not your legal right to ask for a refund after 30 days from buying a faulty item, you can still ask for a repair or replacement. And some shops may want to provide good customer service by giving you a refund anyway, so it's worth asking.

- Your rights are worse if you buy online.

  FALSE: Online traders must abide by the Consumer Rights Act as well. However, if you buy from a private trader, for example on eBay, you only have rights if the seller lies about the product.

How to make a complaint

It's all very well having rights, but how do you put them into effect when something you buy is faulty or inadequate?

1. Return the faulty item to the shop within 30 days. Politely but firmly ask the shop assistant for a refund or replacement.

   OK?

   ↓ NO

2. Say that it is your right under the Consumer Rights Act 2015. If necessary, ask for the supervisor or manager, and say you will take the matter further.

   OK?

   ↓ NO

3. Send a complaint to the company's head office. Describe what action you've taken and what you want the company to do. Or use the free online Resolver service if you bought the item from one of the 870 companies covered by Resolver.

   OK?

   ↓ NO

4. Warn the seller that you will take legal action by a certain date. After that date, contact Citizens Advice. This organisation will help you take the company to the small claims court.

WRITE

Draw up a list stating when you are entitled to a refund, for example: '1. When the item is bad quality …' Then write another list stating when you are *not* entitled to a refund. Swap your lists with a partner's and see if you can change or add anything.

ROLE PLAY

You have bought some trainers in a sale at a high-street store. After a week, you notice that the sole is coming away slightly on one of them.

- In pairs, role play taking the goods back to the shop. One of you is the customer, the other is a helpful and well-informed shop assistant.

- Then swap roles, but this time with the shop assistant being rude and unhelpful.

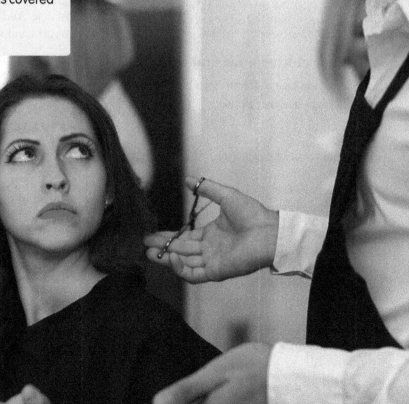

15.2 Financial choices

How we choose to use our money has an impact on everyone – ourselves, others and the wider world.

Thinking carefully about our choices makes us financially responsible consumers.

YOUR CHOICE

Read the following statements about money. Which do you agree with and which do you disagree with? Give your reasons.

> Never borrow money under any circumstances.

> If you look after the pennies, the pounds will look after themselves.

> Never buy on impulse. Research before you buy.

> Paying more for big brands is a waste of money.

> It's a shop's job to make money out of you, so you have to watch out.

> If you lend money to your friends, you will lose your friends.

> You can always rely on your parents or carers to help you out.

Designer clothes – for and against

Mark and Lola have different views about buying – and wearing – designer clothes.

FOR

All clothes are designed, aren't they, so the issue here is about well-made, stylish clothes. What's wrong with that?

Designer brands have to be made to certain standards. That usually means they will not exploit low-paid workers – unlike clothes made in sweatshops. They are often eco-friendly too.

How teenagers look is really important for our confidence. If we feel good in a well-made brand then why knock it?

You can often buy designer clothes more cheaply in sales or by shopping around. Anyway, as long as you can afford it (or your parents or carers can), then you shouldn't feel guilty about it.

AGAINST

Buying designer clothes is not cool. In fact, it's cooler to be an individual than to look the same as everyone else. Develop your own style by finding out what looks good on you rather than on anyone else.

If you took the logo off your shirt or trainers, you wouldn't be able to distinguish them from many other cheaper brands. So why pay extra just for snob value?

Fashions change when clothes companies want to make more money out of you. Charity shops have great vintage clothes and classic clothes don't go out of date. And sharing clothes with friends is fun as well as great value for money.

You are paying a lot of money to walk around advertising for a big clothes company. Shouldn't they be paying you? Who is really winning here?

WRITE

Read the article 'Designer clothes – for and against'. Do you agree with Mark or with Lola? Are there any other points you would add to their argument? Write a short statement of your views on buying and wearing designer clothes.

DISCUSS

In groups, collect ideas on how to look good for less money.

Your responsibilities as a consumer

As a consumer, you have responsibilities as well as rights. Consumer responsibility means taking into account the social and ethical factors that go into producing or selling the goods that we choose to buy.

Why buy ethically?

Whatever we buy – whether everyday food and goods or bigger purchases such as holidays and cars – there is always a hidden cost. Buying cheap clothes which have been made in sweatshops is a vote for worker exploitation. Buying a gas guzzling 4×4, especially if you are a city dweller, is a vote for climate change.

Factory farmed animals, meanwhile, may make cheap meat but it comes at a price on the quality of life of the animal. When it comes to shopping at supermarkets, the cost can be to our high streets and local shops.

Even small, everyday purchases, such as coffee, tea, breakfast cereal, bread or bin-bags are a vote for something. Favouring organic produce is a vote for environmental sustainability and Fairtrade is a vote for human rights.

As consumers, we have a great deal of power in our pockets. Just look at how the supermarkets and food companies responded on the issue of genetically modified food. Even the threat of withdrawing our custom can change company policy.

Considering ethical issues when we go shopping means taking impacts like this into account.

Ethical Consumer website, 2018

What is Fairtrade?

Fairtrade is a way of protecting workers around the world from being exploited by companies. It also protects poorer countries from being exploited by richer ones. The Fairtrade mark on goods means that:

- farmers have been offered a fair price for their produce
- workers' rights have to be respected in the companies

- they have been farmed in an ecologically friendly way
- some of the profit is invested into projects to improve local healthcare, schooling and so on.

Buying Fairtrade, therefore, means that you can help to make the world a fairer place.

DISCUSS

1. Read the article 'Why buy ethically?' Take each of the items in turn (from 'cheap clothes' to 'Fairtrade') and discuss what good or bad effects on society or the environment may result from buying the goods.

2. Are there any products you do not buy because of your principles or beliefs?

3. Do you know anyone who does not buy certain products or services because of their beliefs?

RESEARCH

1. Explore the Fairtrade website. Choose one product, for example bananas, and discover what it means for the farmers and their communities if you buy Fairtrade.

2. Find out how to become a Fairtrade school. If you are already a Fairtrade school, think about how you personally could raise the profile of Fairtrade even further.

YOUR CHOICE

Shopping ethically is not straightforward. There may be a dilemma – a clash in principles. Where do you stand on the following two dilemmas?

1. 'Buying Fairtrade supports farmers in the less industrialised economies of the world, but it means local producers may lose out. And goods from abroad have to be transported long distances, which damages the environment.'

2. 'If you buy cheap goods, that makes you a "responsible consumer" because you are not over-spending. But producers of cheap goods often exploit their workers to drive the price down.'

16.1 Climate change

Climate change is the fact that our climate is changing more rapidly now than it has during any other period in recorded human history.

There is a debate among politicians about what is causing climate change. Is it part of a natural cycle, or is it caused by humans? Most scientists researching the issue globally (97 per cent of them) believe that it is caused by human activity. This hasn't stopped some politicians, like Donald Trump, denying that climate change is primarily caused by human beings.

If we do not take action, the average global temperature will rise by 3°C before the end of the 21st century. This will mean that sea levels will rise by an average of at least 1.2 metres and extensive flooding will become more common. We are already seeing more extreme weather events, such as the wildfires in California in 2018, stronger hurricanes in the Caribbean and stronger typhoons in the Pacific Ocean.

RESEARCH

Research Donald Trump or another politician who denies climate change.

- What have they said on the issue?
- Why do you think it suits them to deny climate change caused by human beings, when the overwhelming evidence suggests that it is?

Give reasons for your views.

Global warming

The major problem connected with climate change is global warming. This is the long-term average rise in global temperatures. Global warming is caused by the gases we release when burning fossil fuels, such as oil, petrol, diesel and gas. These release greenhouse gases, the most problematic of which is carbon dioxide (CO_2). Greenhouse gases allow the Sun's energy to reach the Earth's surface, but prevent it from leaking back out into space. The result is that the Earth heats up like a greenhouse (see the diagram below).

Case study – The Maldives

The Maldives is a collection of over 1000 islands to the south-east of India. They are low-lying atolls, the remains of volcanoes, some of which lie just above the water. No land anywhere in the Maldives is more than 5 metres above the water. Despite this, there are 200 populated islands for locals, and another 100 islands that contain luxury hotels. Tourism is a major industry in the Maldives.

Some of the islands are very densely populated. There are over 430 000 people living in the Maldives, and hundreds of thousands of tourists visit every year. Yet sea level rises are putting the entire country under threat. Experts have predicted that because of global warming and climate change, the entire country could be underwater in 30 to 40 years, unless we change our behaviour by burning less of the fossil fuels that are contributing to global warming and rising sea levels.

OZONE LAYER
GREENHOUSE GASES

Look at the following statements. Which ones do you agree with? Give reasons for your views.

1. We have a moral obligation to future generations to leave the planet at least in the same state it is currently in.

2. Taking action is pointless unless everyone does it. If we stop emissions of polluting CO_2, but China and the USA don't, it will make no real difference.

3. What is happening in the Maldives is genocide – we are wiping out an entire country and their traditions with our actions.

4. The Maldives are part of the problem. We can't keep flying there on planes, which are one of the biggest polluters of greenhouse gases in our atmosphere. The Maldives themselves will have to change.

Air pollution

Climate change is not the only problem caused by air pollution. The air we breathe is also becoming polluted with chemicals and gases that are produced as a result of human activity. Air pollution from traffic is one of the main causes of asthma in the UK, and leads to thousands of premature deaths each year. Chemicals in the air can also cause skin irritation. Chemicals getting into the water system can cause acid rain, which damages trees and forests. Fish in UK canals have been known to change sex because of humanmade chemicals getting into the water. All of this is contributing to species extinction (see below).

Case study – Southampton's polluted air

Southampton is one of 10 cities in the UK with the most polluted air, with air quality at dangerous levels. It is estimated than each year over 80 people die in Southampton just due to polluted air. This is a combination of air pollution from traffic and from diesel engines used to power container and cruise ships at Southampton docks. Several solutions have been proposed, including a congestion charge zone (similar to the one in London) to reduce traffic, and building an electrical infrastructure so that container and cruise ships have to draw electricity from the national grid (known as plug at port) rather than running expensive and polluting diesel engines while in dock.

Imagine you are responsible for running Southampton's environmental department at the local council.

1. In groups, think about the following questions:

- Which would you prioritise – economic growth, or sorting out the polluted air?

- If you decide to prioritise air pollution, what are you going to do? Bear in mind that introducing a congestion charge might harm local businesses, and introducing plug at port means somebody will have to pay for building the infrastructure.

2. Decide what you are going to do, who is going to pay for it and how, for example through fines, taxes or voluntary contributions. Give reasons for your decisions.

Species extinction

Due to human activity since the industrial revolution, species are becoming extinct at an alarming rate. This means animals and plants are dying out because the local area where they live, known as their natural habitat, is disappearing. This can be caused by sea levels rising, ice melting, forests being cut down for wood, farmers taking over more land for growing crops, and more roads and houses being built. Often there is a chain reaction – when one species is lost, other species that depend on it go into decline as well.

Research examples of species extinction in a particular area or country, such as the number of bird species that are declining in Wales.

1. How much species extinction is occurring there?

2. What can be done to alleviate the problem?

16.2 Dealing with climate change

There are many different solutions to climate change, including sustainable development, reducing our energy consumption, reducing our food consumption, and protecting our natural resources.

Sustainable development

Sustainable development is when we take the environment into account. We do this by coming up with developments that protect the environment and reduce our impact on it. We can do this by:

- using natural renewable resources instead of scarce irreplaceable ones (such as coal, oil and gas)

- not damaging the environment, so that we can maintain biodiversity – the number and different species that live in a particular area.

Case study – plastic

Plastic pollution is now a major threat to our health. Plastic is produced from oil, another non-renewable resource. It is used everywhere, for example, to package our food, and to make disposable cartons, cups, straws and cutlery.

The problem with many plastics is that they don't biodegrade – break down to become part of the natural environment. Instead, plastics go into landfill or enter our water supply and are eaten by fish and marine animals. This contributes to species extinction and is also making us ill.

Scientists are looking for ways to reduce plastic pollution, including using more types of recyclable plastic.

DISCUSS

1. In pairs, look around the room you are sitting in. How many items can you see that are made of plastic? What substitutes are available?

2. What one thing will you do next week to reduce your use of single-use plastic?

RESEARCH

Using the internet, including news websites such as the *Guardian*, *Independent* or *Telegraph*, research the latest techniques scientists are looking at to break down plastic in the natural environment. How much progress have they made?

Sustainable solutions

In order to reduce climate change and mass pollution, sustainable development needs to take place on a global scale. There are several different areas where this is needed.

Energy consumption

Energy consumption is already changing as the world supply of oil diminishes. However, we are still too dependent on fossil fuels (coal, oil and natural gas) in the industrialised world. Also, as less industrialised countries progress, they are beginning to use more energy.

There are two main solutions. One is to use nuclear energy. This avoids producing the greenhouse gases that contribute to global warming. However, critics of nuclear energy argue that a lot of CO_2 is produced in constructing the nuclear power plants. Worse still is the spent radioactive fuel, which has to be stored for hundreds of years. Campaigners against nuclear power have argued that all we are doing is transferring a pollution problem from our generation to future generations.

An alternative is renewable energy. This comes, for example from wind farms, wave farms and hydro-electric plants (where power is produced from water flowing downhill). The natural energy from wind, waves and running water is collected using a turbine, which then produces electricity. These are very clean forms of power. Denmark produced 44 per cent of its electricity from wind last year. None the less, some campaigners in the UK have protested against wind farms, saying that they spoil the natural landscape.

Solar energy, from the sun, can also be used to create electricity through solar panels. This is particularly effective in hotter countries, like Africa and Australia. In the UK, some households have become micro-generators of energy, using solar panels and wind turbines to reduce their electricity bills.

YOUR CHOICE

Consider the alternative forms of energy discussed above. Which ones do you or would you use? Give reasons for your views.

Food and water consumption

Large amounts of energy, water, land and other natural resources are consumed across the world to generate food for the planet. However, different types of food use different amounts of natural resources. It is estimated that producing meat takes up two and a half times as much land as producing food for a vegetarian diet, and five times as much land as producing plants for a vegan diet. Therefore, one solution would be to eat less meat.

More pesticides and herbicides have been used to improve the amount of food that can be generated on the land. However, these chemicals are very harmful to some forms of wildlife, particularly bees, and contribute to species extinction. We depend on the bees to pollinate our plants and flowers each year.

Another solution has been to develop genetically modified (GM) crops, which produce more food on the same amount of land. However, campaigners against GM crops say we don't know the health effects of such crops in the long run.

DISCUSS

What do you think should be done to limit the resources we use for food consumption?

- Should we eat less meat? Would you be willing to go meat free for one or two days a week?
- How about becoming vegan or vegetarian? How might this help?

Give reasons for your views.

Protecting natural resources

Natural resources are disappearing at an alarming rate around the planet. Trees are cut down on a massive scale for their wood. It is estimated that an area the size of Wales is lost to deforestation in the Amazon each year, as the trees are cut down for timber and to increase farmland. Sometimes the land is used to produce soya beans, the very thing needed for a vegan diet. So there are competing environmental claims on the land.

One solution is sustainable forestry, which means making sure new trees are planted to replace old ones. So if trees take 20 years to mature, you only cut down one twentieth of the trees, or 5 per cent each year.

RESEARCH

Using the internet, research what is being done in Scotland to manage its natural wood resources.

16.3 Poverty

Poverty is when your income is so low that you cannot meet your basic needs of food, water, shelter and security.

Poverty and more industrialised countries

A more industrialised country is one that has a well-developed infrastructure, such as roads, electricity, schools and hospitals. Many, but not all, of these countries are western democracies, such as the UK, USA, Canada, Australia, New Zealand and the countries within the European Union. However, there are other countries, such as Japan, that are more economically developed.

Poverty can still occur in these countries. The poverty line is the amount of money a person needs for a basic standard of living in a particular country. In the UK, it is estimated that more than 1 in 4 children live below the poverty line. This means they may live in a house where the heating isn't switched on every day in winter, they may have to wear clothes or shoes that don't fit, or they may miss meals sometimes because their parents or carers cannot afford the food.

Relative poverty is a measure of how one person's wealth relates to the average in that country. In countries where wealth is unequal, there will be more relative poverty, even though the country as a whole may look rich. In the UK, relative poverty has been increasing in recent years.

People in relative poverty may use their savings in the short term to see them through (if they have any), but may still have problems in the long term. They are not able to do activities such as having a nice meal out, going to the cinema to see the latest film, buying birthday presents or going on holiday.

Fact check

One charity, the Joseph Rowntree Foundation, has come up with a new definition of poverty, which includes one-off savings that have been used up. Using this, they have calculated that poverty in the UK was as follows in September 2018:

- 14.2 million people are in poverty, including 4.5 million children, 8.4 million working-age adults, and 1.4 million pensioners.

- Nearly half of people locked into poverty (6.9 million) are disabled themselves or live in a family with someone who is.

- One in eight people in the UK is in persistent poverty: they are in poverty now and have been in poverty in at least two of the previous three years. Persistent poverty is highest for those in workless families and disabled families.

- Around 8.2 million people are more than 25 per cent below the poverty line, and 2.5 million people are less than 10 per cent above it.

DISCUSS

1. What do you think life is like without a fridge, a cooker or a washing machine? How would it affect a person on a daily basis?

2. Look at the information above. Are there any figures that surprise you? Why?

Poverty and less economically developed countries

A less economically developed country is one that hasn't completed its industrial revolution. These countries are mainly found in Africa and Asia. Over 80 per cent of the world's population live in a less industrialised country. These people earn less than 20 per cent of the world's income. According to the World Bank, 1.3 billion people live in extreme poverty, on less than $1.25 per day. This figure has fallen by 0.1 billion since 2008, but there is still a long way to go.

Monique's story

Monique lives in Ethiopia, in Africa. Each day she has to walk several miles, twice a day, to get water for her family. The water is very heavy, but she has learned to take turns carrying it with each arm and having a break every mile. The water is dirty, so there is always a risk of picking up a disease from it. Monique's sister died last year from a waterborne infection.

The problem in Ethiopia and neighbouring Sudan has been going on for 30 years, since the rains started to fail more frequently in East Africa. This is thought to be part of climate change caused by global warming. The failure of the rains also means that people can't grow their crops to eat and sell. This has made real poverty worse in these countries.

Charities have tried to help the region. At first they provided food and medical supplies. In the long run, charities like Water Aid have tried to build more wells, so that people have their own supply of fresh drinking water locally.

Monique doesn't have any electricity, but her family now has a wind-up lamp donated by the government. This means that they get some light in the evening. They also have a clockwork radio so they can listen to news and music.

DISCUSS

In pairs, imagine living in a country where you had to walk five miles for clean water every day, or only had electricity for two hours a day. How would your life be different from the one you live in the UK? Give reasons for your views.

Relative poverty in less industrialised countries

Some less industrialised countries have a small, wealthy elite but a far less wealthy general population, some of whom live in absolute poverty. Sometimes, these elites survive through corruption, political oppression and violence. In these cases, poverty is just one of a number of problems that people in that country have to deal with.

RESEARCH

Using the internet and articles from the BBC website and the *Guardian* newspaper, research Zimbabwe. What problems has the country had in recent years that have contributed to poverty there?

DISCUSS

In groups, imagine you are a parent or carer who only has £3 a day left after paying essential bills and buying essential items (for example, school uniform and food for your children). What would be the most sensible things to do with the money?

16.4 Genetic engineering

Genes are the building blocks of life. They are a set of chemicals that is in every cell of every living thing to programme what that cell does.

Genetically modified (GM) crops

With advances in genetic engineering, it has now become possible to genetically modify (change) crops. This means scientists can take part of one gene that is really resistant to diseases and place it in a different plant from a different species to make it more disease resistant. This is only one of many examples of changes that can be made to plants and animals to make them healthier and produce more.

However, opponents of genetically modified foods call these 'Frankenstein foods', after the monster created by Dr Frankenstein in Mary Shelley's novel. Organisations such as Greenpeace are worried about the long-term safety of such foods. They argue that once a GM crop is released into the environment, it is out there for good and cannot be recalled.

There have been some trial sites to grow GM crops in the UK but, because of concerns about them, commercial growing of GM crops is not permitted. However, GM crops are allowed to come into the UK to be used as animal feed.

Opposition to GM foods has been so strong in the UK that sometimes activists have taken direct action. This has included tearing up and destroying GM crops on the trial sites, so that they do not contaminate the environment.

Modified progress

They bred the seed. They fed the seed.
They nurtured it with care.
They promised a bumper harvest
For all the world to share.

They piled it high upon the shelves.
It glowed with health outside.
But who knows where the changes stop
When crops are modified.

John Foster

DISCUSS

1. Do you think it was right for Greenpeace activists to tear up the GM crops? Or can illegal direct action never be justified? Give reasons for your views.

2. How aware are you of whether any of the food you eat is GM? Explain your answer.

3. Is there is a moral difference between changing the way a vegetable grows and changing how a cow develops? Explain your opinion.

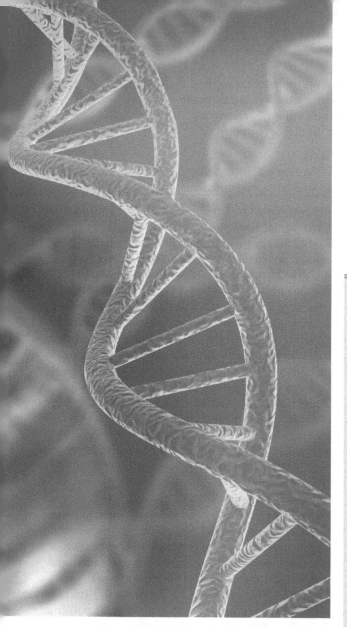

Scientists have great hopes for cloning. Already, the world's first burger using cloned meat has been produced, leading some to speculate we could grow our own meat in the future, reducing the need to kill animals. Scientists are also experimenting on growing individual human organs, such as a liver, in the laboratory. The hope is that one day scientists will be able to grow healthy organs for those needing an organ transplant, which will save millions of lives globally each year.

Case study – Genetically modified babies

Scientists are also hoping to use genetic editing to avoid genetic diseases. In the UK in 2018, scientists in Newcastle were given permission to start experiments, with the aim of producing a baby that would be born from the genetic material of three parents. Over 99 per cent of the genetic material would come from the biological parents. Less than 1 per cent would come from another woman, to replace any faulty DNA causing a whole range of genetic diseases.

Opponents of these experiments argue against them on a variety of grounds. These include the unknown effects in the long run to the babies, and religious grounds, saying scientists do not have the right to play God. Opponents also argue that genetic modification will end up being used in a frivolous way, for example to produce babies with only blonde hair or blue eyes, or to determine a baby's sex (which is against the law).

DISCUSS

Do you think the UK government should allow genetically modified babies to be born?

Give reasons for your views.

RESEARCH

Using the internet, find out the latest developments in the UK and China regarding genetically modified babies.

Cloning

Our genetic sequence is made up of DNA, the structure of which was discovered in 1953. In 1990, the Human Genome Project was launched. The idea was to map all of the DNA in a human cell. This would make it easier to manipulate genes, a process known as genetic engineering. The project was completed two years early in 2003.

Cloning is a process where the DNA in a cell is taken from one living thing, and an identical copy is grown. This is initially done in a laboratory. In 1996, the world's first living cloned sheep, Dolly, was created in the UK by scientists at the University of Edinburgh.

Acknowledgments

The publishers gratefully acknowledge the permission granted to reproduce the copyright material in this book. Every effort has been made to trace copyright holders and to obtain their permission for the use of copyright material. The publishers will gladly receive any information enabling them to rectify any error or omission at the first opportunity.

Images

Key: t = top, b = bottom, l = left, r = right, c = centre.

p7 Larry St. Pierre/Shutterstock Shutterstock, p8 fizkes/Shutterstock, p9 DGLimages/Shutterstock, p11 Monkey Business Images/Shutterstock, p13 kaisaya/Shutterstock, p14 l Kzenon/Shutterstock, p14 r kipgodi/Shutterstock, p15 Rawpixel.com/Shutterstock, p16 Barabasa/Shutterstock, p17 Beepstock/Alamy Stock Photo, p19 Ira Berger/Alamy Stock Photo, p21 l EFE News Agency/Alamy Stock Photo, p21 r Oleh Dubyna/Shutterstock, p22 MBI/Alamy Stock Photo, p23 Antonio Guillem/Shutterstock, p24 The poster 'I don't' from Karma Nirvana and West Yorkshire Police, www.westyorkshire.police.uk/forcedmarriage. Reproduced with permission, p27 Twocoms/Shutterstock, p30 Jack Taylor/Stringer/Getty Images, pp34–35 Samuel Borges Photography/Shutterstock, p36 Mediscan/Alamy Stock Photo, p39 accem/Shutterstock, p40 Diego Cervo/Shutterstock, p43 Barabasa/Shutterstock, p44 John Birdsall/Alamy Stock Photo, p45 Chris Rout/Alamy Stock Photo, p46 cl michaeljung/Shutterstock, p46 tr Syda Productions/Shutterstock, p46b New Africa/Shutterstock, p47 Valentina Razumova/Shutterstock, p48 See Li/Alamy Stock Photo, p49 Milind Arvind Ketkar/Shutterstock, pp50–51 Dean Drobot/Shutterstock, p52 goldeneden/Shutterstock, p53 Image Courtesy of The Advertising Archives, p54 Daxiao Productions/Shutterstock, p56 sashafolly/Shutterstock, p60 l Pool/Pool/Getty Images, p60 r Lexington Herald-Leader/Contributor/Getty Images, p62 luckat/Shutterstock, p65 weedezign/Shutterstock, p66 Monkey Business Images/Shutterstock, p68 4Max/Shutterstock, p73 Oleg Golovnev/Shutterstock, p75 Iakov Filimonov/Shutterstock, p76 Photographee.eu/Shutterstock, p79 Igor_Koptilin/Shutterstock, p80 Dean Drobot/Shutterstock, p81 Nick Moore/Alamy Stock Photo, p83 Silvi Photo/Shutterstock, p85 Iakov Filimonov/Shutterstock, p86 l stockyimages/Shutterstock, p86 r Pop Paul-Catalin/Shutterstock, p87 Thinglass/Shutterstock, p88 l VectorMine/Shutterstock, p88 r Sven Hansche/Shutterstock, p90 Rich Carey/Shutterstock, p91 l Steve Meese/Shutterstock, p91 r lightrain/Shutterstock, p92 Trevor Chriss/Alamy Stock Photo, p93 Martchan/Shutterstock, p94 Steve Morgan/Alamy Stock Photo, p95 Billion Photos/Shutterstock.

Texts

We are grateful to the following for permission to reproduce copyright material:

Extracts on pp.11, 71 from Mind Your Head by Juno Dawson, Hot Key Books, 2016, pp.33-35, 83-84. Reproduced by permission of Bonnier Zaffre; An extract on p.16 from "The Man Box" by Tony Porter, A Call to Men, www.acalltomen.org. Reproduced with permission; An extract on p.23 after Michelle, http://www.safelives.org.uk/news-views/real-life-stories/michelle. Reproduced with permission of SafeLives; An extract on p.24 from the charity Karma Nirvana, https://karmanirvana.org.uk. Reproduced with permission; An extract on p.31 from "Institutional racism still plagues policing, warns chief constable" by Vikram Dodd, The Guardian, 12/10/2018, copyright © Guardian News & Media Ltd 2019; The poem on p.47 "What is a mother?" by Mary M. Donoghue, published in Smells of Childhood, Brewin Books, 1997. Reproduced with permission of the publisher; An extract on p.63 from "Intervention working". Reproduced with permission from Educate Against Hate, https://educateagainsthate.com; The figure on p.70 "Mental Health Spectrum tool", Centre for Mental Health, www.centreformentalhealth.org.uk. Reproduced with permission; An extract on p.81 from "400,000 British teens lured into under-aged gambling through video games, investigation reveal", The Daily Telegraph, 28/06/2018, copyright © Telegraph Media Group Limited 2018; and an extract on p.87 from "Why Buy Ethically?", http://www.ethicalconsumer.org, copyright © Ethical Consumer. Reproduced with permission.

Every effort has been made to trace the copyright holders and obtain permission to reproduce material in this book. Please do get in touch with any enquiries or any information.